ACE YOUR **BIOLOGY SCIENCE PROJECT**

ACE YOUR SCIENCE PROJECT ABOUT THE SENSES

Robert Gardner, Thomas R. Rybolt,
Leah M. Rybolt, and Barbara Gardner Conklin

GREAT SCIENCE FAIR IDEAS

Enslow Publishers, Inc.
40 Industrial Road
Box 398
Berkeley Heights, NJ 07922
USA
http://www.enslow.com

Library of Congress Cataloging-in-Publication Data

Gardner, Robert, 1929–
    Ace your science project about the senses : great science fair ideas / Robert Gardner . . . [et al.],
       p. cm. — (Ace your biology science project)
    Includes bibliographical references and index.
    Summary: "Presents several science projects and science project ideas
       about the senses"—Provided by publisher.
    ISBN-13: 978-0-7660-3217-0
    ISBN-10: 0-7660-3217-5
    1. Senses and sensation—Experiments—Juvenile literature. 2. Science projects—Juvenile
       literature. 3. Science fairs—Juvenile literature. I. Gardner, Robert, 1929–
    QP434.A24 2010
    612.8—dc22
                                     2008030797
Printed in the United States of America

10 9 8 7 6 5 4 3 2 1

To Our Readers: We have done our best to make sure all Internet Addresses in this book were active and appropriate when we went to press. However, the author and the publisher have no control over and assume no liability for the material available on those Internet sites or on other Web sites they may link to. Any comments or suggestions can be sent by e-mail to comments@enslow.com or to the address on the back cover.

♻ Enslow Publishers, Inc., is committed to printing our books on recycled paper. The paper in every book contains 10% to 30% post-consumer waste (PCW). The cover board on the outside of each book contains 100% PCW. Our goal is to do our part to help young people and the environment too!

The experiments in this book are a collection of the authors' best experiments, which were previously published by Enslow Publishers, Inc. in *Health Science Projects About Psychology*; *Health Science Projects About Your Senses*; *Science Fair Success with Scents, Aromas, and Smells*; *Science Projects About Sound*; and *Soda Pop Science Projects*.

Illustration Credits: Stephen F. Delisle, Figures 4, 5, 6, 7, 8, 9, 10, 11, 12, 13, 15, 16, 17, 18, 19, 20, 23, 24, 25; Enslow Publishers, Inc., Figures 2, 3, 14, 21, 26; LifeART image copyright 1988 Lippincott Williams & Wilkins. All rights reserved, Figure 1; Tom LaBaff, Figure 22.

Photos Credits: © bubaone/iStockphoto.com, trophy icons; © Chen Fu Soh/iStockphoto.com, backgrounds; Shutterstock, collage, p 10.

Cover Photos: © Peter Chen/iStockphoto.com (boy); Shutterstock (items).

CONTENTS

CHAPTER 1

Vision 11

CHAPTER 2

The Sense of Hearing 43

CHAPTER 3

The Sense of Smell 62

CHAPTER 4

The Sense of Taste 82

❶ Indicates experiments that offer ideas for science fair projects.

☻ *Indicates experiments that offer ideas for science fair projects.*

INTRODUCTION

When you hear the word *science*, do you think of a person in a white lab coat surrounded by beakers of bubbling liquids, specialized lab equipment, and computers? What exactly is science? Maybe you think science is only a subject you learn in school. Science is much more than this.

Science studies the things that are all around you, every day. No matter where you are or what you are doing, scientific principles are at work. You don't need special materials or equipment, or even a white lab coat, to be a scientist. Materials commonly found in your home, at school, or at a local store will allow you to become a scientist and pursue an area of interest. By making careful observations and asking questions about how things work, you can begin to design experiments to investigate a variety of questions. You can do science. You probably already have but just didn't know it!

Perhaps you are reading this book because you are looking for an idea for a science fair project for school, or maybe you are just hoping to find something fun to do on a rainy day. This book will provide an opportunity for you to learn about your senses and carry out experiments involving vision, hearing, taste, smell, and touch. Sensory organs include the eye, the ear, the tongue, the nose, and receptors in the skin. These gather information from your environment and send it to your brain where it is processed. It is a complex process to understand. It involves not only biology, but chemistry and physics too. Undoubtedly you will discover how much fun it is to experiment with the senses.

THE SCIENTIFIC METHOD

All scientists look at the world and try to understand how things work. They make careful observations and conduct research about a question. Different areas of science use different approaches. Depending on the phenomenon being investigated, one method is likely to be more appropriate than another. Designing a new medication for heart disease, studying the spread of an invasive plant species such as purple loosestrife, and finding evidence about whether there was once water on Mars all require different methods.

Despite the differences, however, all scientists use a similar general approach to do experiments. It is called the scientific method. In most experiments, some or all of the following steps are used: making an observation, formulating a question, making a hypothesis (an answer to the question) and prediction (an if-then statement), designing and conducting an experiment, analyzing results and drawing conclusions, and accepting or rejecting the hypothesis. Scientists then share their findings with others by writing articles that are published in journals. After—and only after—a hypothesis has repeatedly been supported by experiments can it be considered a theory.

You might be wondering how to get an experiment started. When you observe something in the world, you may become curious and think of a question. Your question can be answered by a well-designed investigation. Your question may also arise from an earlier experiment or from background reading. Once you have a question, you should make a hypothesis. Your hypothesis is a possible answer to the question (what you think will happen). Once you have a hypothesis, it is time to design an experiment.

In some cases, it is appropriate to do a controlled experiment. This means there are two groups treated exactly the same except for the single factor that you are testing. That factor is often called a variable. For example, if you want to investigate whether the sense of smell influences taste, two groups may be used. One group is called the control group, and the other is called the experimental group. Tasting foods with the nose plugged will form the control group, while tasting without plugging the nose will be the experimental group. The variable is the plugged or unplugged nose—it is the thing that changes, and it is the only difference between the two groups. The two groups should be treated exactly the same: The subjects should taste the same types of food, and it should be cut into chunks of the same size and shape. The nose should be plugged in the same way, and the subjects should chew the chunks in the same way.

During the experiment, you will collect data. For example, you might determine how many of the foods are tasted and identified accurately. By comparing the data collected from the control group with the data collected from the experimental group, you will draw conclusions. Since the two groups were treated exactly alike, you could conclude with confidence that any difference between the groups is a result of the one thing that was different: an unplugged nose.

Two other terms that are often used in scientific experiments are *dependent* and *independent* variables. The dependent variable here is the ability to taste, because it depends upon the sense of smell. Sense of smell is the independent variable (it doesn't depend on anything). After the data is collected, it is analyzed to see whether the hypothesis was true or false. Often, the results of one experiment will lead you to a related question, or they may send you off in a different direction. Whatever the results, there is something to be learned from all scientific experiments.

SCIENCE FAIRS

Many of the experiments in this book may be appropriate for science fair projects. Experiments marked with an asterisk (🔻) include a section called Science Fair Project Ideas. The ideas in this section will provide suggestions to help you develop your own original science fair project. However, judges at such fairs do not reward projects or experiments that are simply copied from a book. For example, a model of an ear or an eye, which is commonly found at these fairs, would probably not impress judges unless it was done in a novel or creative way. On the other hand, a carefully performed experiment to find out how smell affects taste would be likely to receive careful consideration.

Science fair judges tend to reward creative thought and imagination. However, it's difficult to be creative or imaginative unless you are really interested in your project. If you decide to do a project, be sure to choose a topic that appeals to you. Consider, too, your own ability and the cost of materials. Don't pursue a project that you can't afford.

If you decide to use a project found in this book for a science fair, you will need to find ways to modify or extend it. This should not be difficult because you will probably find that as you do these projects new ideas for experiments will come to mind. These new experiments could make excellent science fair projects, particularly because they spring from your own mind and are interesting to you.

If you decide to enter a science fair and have never done so before, you should read some of the books listed in the Further Reading section. The books that deal specifically with science fairs will provide plenty of helpful hints and lots of useful information that will enable you to avoid the pitfalls that sometimes plague first-time entrants. You will learn how to prepare appealing reports that include charts and graphs, how to set up and display your work, how to present your project, and how to relate to judges and visitors.

SAFETY FIRST

As with many activities, safety is important in science, and certain rules apply when conducting experiments. Some of the rules below may seem obvious to you, but each is important to follow.

1. Have **an adult** help you whenever the book advises.

2. Wear eye protection and closed-toe shoes (rather than sandals) and tie back long hair.

3. Don't eat or drink while doing experiments and never taste substances being used unless instructed to do so.

4. Avoid touching chemicals.

5. If either you or a volunteer helping you suffers from allergies, migraine headaches triggered by odors, or asthma, do not use any foods or objects that can cause medical problems.

6. Never smell hazardous products such as ammonia, bleach, gasoline, kerosene, or solvents. Do not breathe the fumes of other household products such as airplane glue, nail polish remover, or paint.

7. Do only those experiments that are described in the book or those that have been approved by **an adult**.

8. Never engage in horseplay or play practical jokes.

9. Before beginning, read through the entire experimental procedure to make sure you understand all instructions. Clear all extra items from your work space.

10. At the end of every activity, clean all materials and put them away. Wash your hands thoroughly with soap and water.

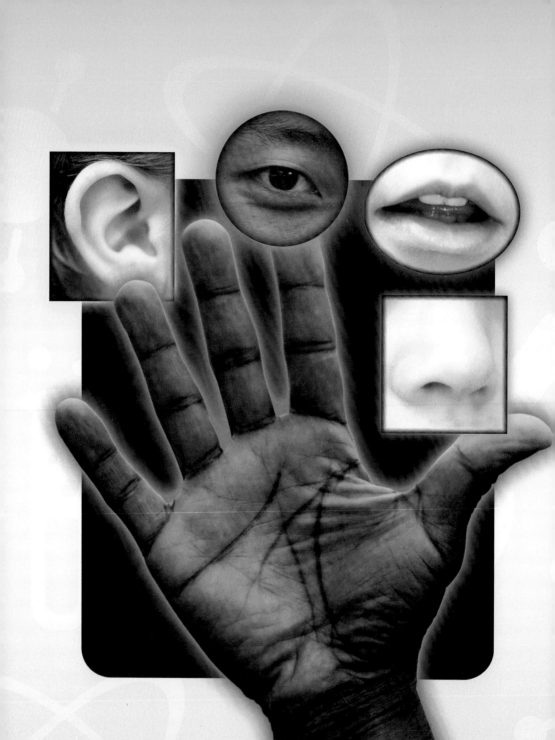

Your five senses are: hearing, sight, taste, smell, and touch.

Chapter 1

Vision

THE HUMAN EYE IS A MAGNIFICENT ORGAN. It enables you to see the world around you, follow the path of a ball thrown to you, read the print in front of you, view the world's greatest art, and see and do a zillion other things. However, without the brain to which your eyes are connected, you would see nothing. For, ultimately, the sense of sight is found not in your eyes but in the rear portion of your brain. It is there that you make sense of the images that register in your eyes.

It is the energy in light that makes vision possible. Photons, the smallest bits of light energy, enter the eyes and stimulate the sensory cells (rod and cone cells) in the eyes that respond to light. The photons that reach the eyes are reflected by, or emitted, from the objects seen. The eyes, despite what you may read in comic strips, do not radiate light. The photons that enter the eyes from visible objects are refracted (bent) by the eyes to form two-dimensional likenesses (images) on the back sides (retinas) of the eyes. The pattern of light in the images stimulates a similar pattern of sensory cells that send nerve impulses to the brain.

THE EYE'S ANATOMY

Figure 1 is a diagram of an eye that has been divided along a vertical plane. (You are looking at a cross section of the eye.) The eye is basically a sphere with what looks like a smaller sphere projecting from its front side.

[FIGURE 1]

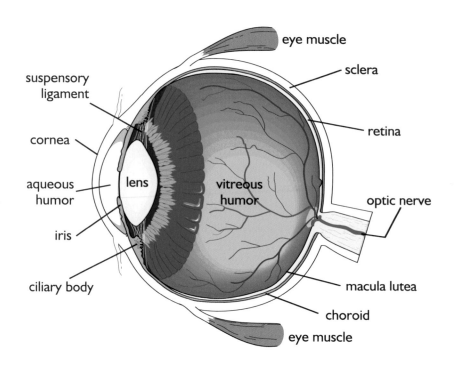

eye muscle

sclera

retina

suspensory ligament

cornea

aqueous humor

lens

vitreous humor

optic nerve

iris

ciliary body

macula lutea

choroid

eye muscle

A diagram of the eye reveals a structure somewhat similar to a camera. Both have a lens. Images in a camera form on film or on a digital sensor array at the back of the camera. In the eye, images fall on the retina. A camera has a shutter that opens to allow light to enter. The eye has an iris with an opening in its center (the pupil) through which light enters the eye.

The interior of the eye is divided into two parts. The space in front of the lens is filled with a watery fluid called the *aqueous humor*. The larger space behind the lens contains a somewhat thicker liquid known as the *vitreous humor*. The vitreous humor is enclosed in a thin membrane that fills the bulk of the space within the eyeball. The vitreous humor maintains the eye's spherical shape in the same way that pressurized air keeps a basketball distended.

The eye has three separate coats. The outer coat is the white of the eye, or *sclera*. It covers five-sixths of the eyeball. It is a firm, thick, fibrous membrane that protects the delicate parts of the eye that lie within it. The front part of the sclera, the part that bulges forward and covers one-sixth of the eyeball, is called the *cornea*. It is transparent so that light can enter the eye.

Look closely at your eye's cornea in a mirror. You may be able to see your own image in your cornea. The cornea is so smooth that it can reflect light just as a curved (convex) mirror does.

There are six muscles outside each eye that are attached to the sclera and to the skull. These muscles hold the eye in its socket and allow you to move your eyes in various directions.

The middle coat, or *choroid*, is a thin, dark membrane that lines the inner surface of the sclera. Just behind the edge of the cornea, the choroid folds inward like a ruffle to form part of the ciliary body. The ciliary body also contains the ciliary muscle, which is attached to the suspensory ligament. When the ciliary muscles contract, the suspensory ligament is less taut and the lens becomes more convex (rounder). When the ciliary muscles relax, the tension on the suspensory ligament increases and the lens becomes less convex.

The lens itself has a yellowish tint so that it acts as a light filter as well as a lens that refracts (bends) light. Were it not for our yellow-tinted lenses, we would see a good portion of the ultraviolet light that is absorbed by the lens.

The front part of the eye's middle coat is the *iris*. It is the circular disk that gives an eye its color—blue, green, gray, brown, or black. At the center of the iris is a circular opening, the *pupil*, which allows light to pass from the cornea to the lens. The size of the pupil is controlled by muscles in the iris that can increase or reduce the pupil's size.

The eye's innermost coat is the *retina*. It contains the receptor cells—rod and cone cells—that respond to light. The light that forms images on the retina stimulates these cells, which send nerve impulses to the brain along the optic nerve. At the center of the retina, about 2 mm from the point where the optic nerve enters each eye, is a region known as the *macula lutea*. Images formed on this part of the retina can be seen very clearly. When you read, your eyes move so that images of the words fall on the center of the macula lutea where the *fovea centralis* is located. Here, in the fovea centralis, each cone cell is connected to a single nerve fiber that carries impulses to the brain's occipital lobe. The occipital lobe is located in the lower, back portion of the brain. In other parts of the retina, several cone or rod cells are connected to a nerve fiber leading to the brain.

🏆 1.1 Forming Images

Materials:
- pencil
- clear glass filled with water
- magnifying glass (convex lens)
- room with a window through which a distant scene can be seen
- a friend
- white index card
- ruler
- lightbulb
- a second lens, more or less convex than the first one

When light enters the eye, it is refracted (bent) as it passes through the cornea, lens, and the fluids that fill the eyeball. You can see that light is refracted as it passes from one substance to another quite easily. Put a pencil in a clear glass filled with water. Notice how the pencil appears to be broken at the point where it enters the water. Light from the pencil that passes through the water before entering the air is bent as it leaves the water. Light from the top of the pencil moves only through air and is not bent.

Actually, the light from the pencil that travels through air is bent, but not until it enters your eyes. There, like all light, it is bent as it passes through your eye.

To see how your eye refracts light to form images on your retina, you can use a magnifying glass (a convex lens) to represent the lens in your eye. The lens can be used to form images of objects outside, such as trees and buildings that you can see through the window of a room. Stand next to a wall opposite the window. The images will be clearer if you turn off lights in the room. Have a friend hold an index card against the end of a ruler (see Figure 2a). The card represents the retina of an eye. Move the lens back and forth along the ruler in front of the card. At some point, light passing through the lens will produce a clear, sharp image of a distant scene that you can see through the window. Is the image right-side-up or upside-down?

When you have a sharp, clear image, what is the distance between the image on the card and the lens? Figure 2b shows what happens to the light rays as they pass through the lens. You can see the light rays are refracted and brought together (converged) by the lens to form an image.

Now repeat the experiment. But this time have your friend hold the card and ruler about a meter (3 feet) from a glowing lightbulb. Use the lens to form a clear image of the bulb on the card. What is the distance between the image and the lens?

Move the lens closer to the bulb in a series of steps. At each point, have your friend move the card until there is a clear image of the bulb. Do you reach a point where it becomes impossible to form a clear image of the bulb?

Slowly move this book closer and closer to your eyes. Do you reach a point where you cannot see the print clearly?

As you probably found, the distance between the lens and a clear image of an object increases as the object moves closer to the lens. How are you able to see objects that are both near and far with equal clarity?

When you focus a good camera, the lens moves farther out or farther in to produce a sharp image on film or on a digital sensor array at the back of the camera. Do our eyeballs lengthen when we look at nearby objects? Do they grow shorter when we look at distant objects?

Our eyeballs fit snugly into their sockets, and we do not see them bulge outward when we look at objects held close to our eyes. Consequently, it is not likely that the shape of our eyeballs changes. How then are we able to see objects that are both near and far?

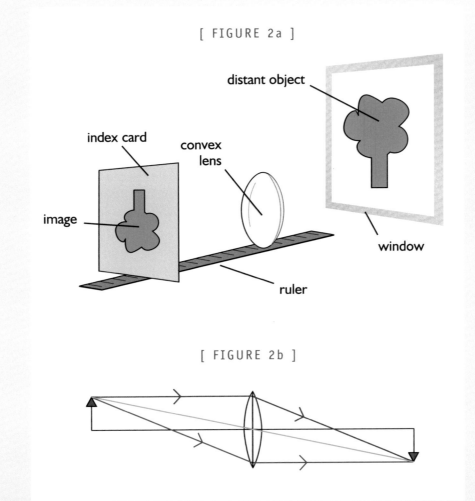

distant object

index card

convex lens

image

window

ruler

[FIGURE 2b]

2 a) **Use a convex lens to form an image on an index card. b) Light rays from the top of an object (arrow) are shown as they approach, pass through, and emerge from a convex lens. The rays are refracted by the lens so that they come back together to form an image. What is shown here for one point of light happens for every point of light reflected from the object. As a result, the image is a replica of the object. Its size, however, depends on the distance of the lens from the object.**

To examine another way in which your eyes might adjust for distance, you will need a second lens. Find one that is more convex (fatter) or less convex (thinner) than the one you used before.

Using this lens, again produce a clear image of a distant object on the white card. Is the distance between the lens and the image the same or different than it was with the first lens?

Use the same lens to produce a clear image of a nearby object on the white card. Is the distance between the lens and the image the same or different than it was with the first lens?

As you can see, lenses that are more convex produce clear images that are closer to the lens. Less convex lenses produce clear images farther from the lens. You cannot slip lenses that are more or less convex into your eyes every time you shift your gaze from near to far or from far to near. However, you can change the convexity of the lenses you have.

When you look at distant objects, your ciliary muscles relax. This increases the tautness of the suspensory ligaments and your lens becomes less convex. As you have seen, distant objects form images closer to a lens of a given convexity. The more convex the lens, the closer to the lens the images form. Reducing the convexity of your lens increases the distance between lens and image so that the image of a faraway object forms on the retina. Under what conditions would you want your ciliary muscles to contract and make your lens more convex?

In fact, your ciliary muscles allow you to adjust the convexity of your lens so that you can form clear images of objects at many different distances from your eyes. What evidence do you have that there is a limit to how convex you can make your lens?

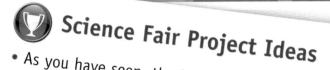

Science Fair Project Ideas

- As you have seen, the images formed by a convex lens are upside down. Why is it that, although the images on our retinas are upside down, we see a world that is right side up?
- What is astigmatism? What is nearsightedness? What is farsightedness? What causes each of these disorders? How can lenses be used to correct these visual problems?
- Investigate a type of surgery called refractive keratomy. Who would need this surgery? Why would they need it?

Materials:

- tape
- square sheet of white paper about 60 cm (2 ft) on a side
- wall or refrigerator door
- black felt-tip pen
- thin white stick or ruler
- a friend
- high-back chair
- meterstick or yardstick
- calculator (optional)

As you learned earlier, the fovea centralis, where you focus images for clearest vision, is at the center of your retina (see Figure 1). Your blind spot, where there are no light-sensitive receptor cells, is near the center of your retina. How far apart are these two small regions of your retina?

To find out, tape a square sheet of paper about 60 cm (2 ft) on a side to a wall or the door of a refrigerator. Use a felt-tip pen to make a small X (about 5 mm or 2 in) at the center of the paper. Use the same pen to make a solid black circle of about the same size as the X near the end of a white stick or ruler.

Have a friend sit in a high-back chair so that his or her right eye is exactly 1.0 meter (39 3/8 in) from the X at the center of the paper and at the same height. The chair's high back will help your friend keep his or her head perfectly still. Ask your friend to close the left eye and focus the right eye on the X. By concentrating on the X, your friend will focus the image of the X on the fovea centralis.

While your friend focuses on the X, hold the stick so that the circle on the stick is close to the X on the paper. Ask your friend to continue to stare at the X as you move the stick with its circle slowly along the paper to your friend's right. Ask your friend to tell you when the circle disappears. When it disappears from your friend's vision, measure and record the distance between the X on the paper and the circle on the stick.

Repeat the experiment several times to be certain the results are consistent. Then repeat the experiment again several times as your friend focuses the left eye on the X with the right eye closed. This time move the circle slowly to the left until its image falls on the blind spot of your friend's left eye.

What is the average distance between the X and the circle when the circle's image falls on the blind spot in your friend's right eye? When it falls on the blind spot in your friend's left eye?

As you can see from the drawing in Figure 3, the distance between the points where the light rays from the X and from the circle fall on the retina (which reaches the blind spot) form the base of a triangle, b, on the retina. The altitude of the triangle, a, is the distance from the retina to the lens of the eye. That small triangle is similar to another triangle whose base, B, is the distance between the X and the circle on the paper. The altitude of this larger triangle, A, is the 1.0 meter distance between the X and the eye of your friend.

Because these two triangles are similar, their sides are proportional. Consequently,

$$\frac{b}{B} = \frac{a}{A}$$

Multiplying both sides of this equation by B gives us

$$\frac{b \times B}{B} = \frac{a \times B}{A}$$

[FIGURE 3]

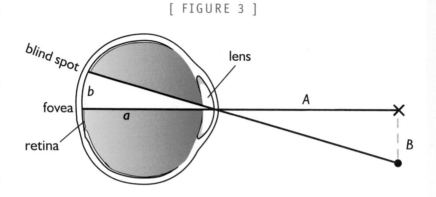

The large triangle with base B and altitude A is similar to the small triangle with base b and altitude a. The small triangle is inside the subject's eye. The base of the big triangle is the distance between the X and the circle when the circle's image lies on the subject's blind spot. The altitude of the big triangle is the distance from the X to the subject's eye.

Since $B \div B = 1$, we have

$$b = \frac{a \times B}{A}$$

Suppose you found the distance, B, between the circle and the X to be 14 cm when the circle's image was on your friend's blind spot. The distance from lens to retina within the eye, a, is approximately 1.5 cm. Your friend's eye was 100 cm from the X. Solving for b, the distance between the blind spot and the fovea, we find

$$b = \frac{a \times B}{A} = \frac{1.5 \text{ cm} \times 14 \text{ cm}}{100 \text{ cm}} = 0.21 \text{ cm, or } 2.1 \text{ mm}$$

From the results of your experiment, what do you find the distance between the blind spot and the fovea to be? Is it the same for both eyes?

Repeat the experiment, but this time you be the subject and let your friend move the stick until the circle falls on your blind spot. How does the distance between your fovea and blind spot compare with that of your friend?

Science Fair Project Idea

Is the distance between fovea and blind spot related to the size of a person's head? Is it related to a person's age? To a person's gender? Design experiments to find out.

Materials:
- a friend
- Ping-Pong ball
- 2 pencils
- ruler

Normally, most people view the world with two eyes. We see a slightly different world with one eye than we do with the other. To see that this is true, lift your right arm and hold it straight out to the side. Then close your left eye and stare straight ahead. How far do you have to move your right arm forward before you can see your right hand with your right eye?

Now close your right eye. How far do you have to move your right arm forward before you can see your right hand with your left eye?

Repeat the experiment using your left arm. Then repeat the experiment for both arms with both eyes open.

As you have seen, your right eye sees more on the right side of your visual field than does your left eye, and vice versa.

DEPTH PERCEPTION

A stereoscopic picture is made by taking two photographs of the same object at slightly different angles and then superimposing one on the other. Such a picture provides a sense of depth. Your eyes automatically provide a stereoscopic picture. The central part of an image falls on corresponding parts of the retinas of both eyes. Your right eye, as you have seen, sees more of an object on the right than does your left eye. Similarly, your left eye sees more of an object on the left than does your right eye. Your brain sees the central part of the image as a single image because the impulses come from corresponding parts of the two retinas. It then adds the extra parts seen only by the right and left eyes to the central part to create an image that provides depth as well as breadth and height.

To compare your perception of depth using one eye and then two, try the following experiments. Begin by playing catch with a friend using a Ping-Pong ball. Do you find it easier to catch the ball when you use two eyes or one?

Next, ask your friend to hold a pencil about 30 cm (1 ft) in front of you about waist high. With both eyes open, try to touch the tip of the pencil with the tip of another pencil that you hold in your dominant hand. Now repeat the experiment with one eye closed. Then try the same experiment with the other eye closed. What evidence do you have that two eyes provide better depth perception than one?

As you have seen, viewing the world through two eyes helps you perceive depth. What other clues or stimuli do we use in perceiving a three-dimensional world?

 Science Fair Project Ideas

- Find out how filmmakers produce movies with three-dimensional effects. Why haven't such movies become popular?
- Roll a sheet of paper into a tube. Look at a distant object with both eyes. Focus your attention so that you perceive just one small part of the object. Now hold the tube in front of one eye and look through it at the same part of the distant object. How might you explain the effect of the tube on your ability to perceive distant objects?

PERCEPTION: CONSTANCY AND ORGANIZATION

Objects tend to be seen as constant even when the stimuli we receive from them are very different. For example, you perceive a professional football player as a large man even though he is no more than several inches tall when viewed from the stands where you sit.

We also tend to organize our perceptions in ways that may be inborn. The genes that we inherit may program the way we perceive things.

FIGURE FROM GROUND

Generally, we can distinguish the essential figure (object) or pattern we see from its background. For example, as you read these words, you do not focus on the white background of the paper but rather on the black print. There are exceptions. Camouflage is used, especially by the military and by nature, to avoid having a figure stand out from the surroundings. And there are reversible figures (see Figure 4a). Reversible figures are carefully designed to provide the brain with two options so that a figure can become the ground and vice versa.

GROUPING

Gestalt psychologists believe many things can be perceived only in their entirety: that the whole is greater than the sum of its parts. They contend that we are born with a tendency to group objects on the basis of similarity, closeness, wholeness, and continuity. Objects similar in shape, size, or color tend to be grouped together (Figure 4b). Stimuli that arise from points close to one another tend to be perceived as belonging together (Figure 4c).

When we see part of an object, we often perceive the whole object. This, Gestalt psychologists say, reveals our tendency to "want" to see things as being whole, although in reality we are seeing only a part of the whole thing.

Similarly, lines that form only part of a figure tend to be seen as a complete figure (see Figure 4d). Motions, such as that of a car moving along a curved path, may be perceived as part of a whole, such as the car's moving in a circle. We expect objects moving along an arc to continue moving in that pattern and, therefore, to follow a circular path even though they may fly off along a tangent if we continue to follow the motion.

What do you see in Figure 4e? You probably see a hat and an X, not four segments. Why? We tend to perceive patterns that are continuous and familiar. You may want to ask some friends or family members what they see in these drawings.

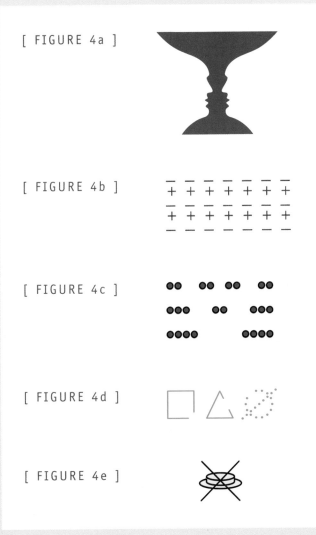

[FIGURE 4a]

[FIGURE 4b]

[FIGURE 4c]

[FIGURE 4d]

[FIGURE 4e]

Examples of a) reversibility, b) similarity, c) closeness, d) wholeness, and e) continuity.

Materials:
- sunlight or bright light in a room
- dark or dimly lighted room
- a night with a star-filled sky
- a friend
- high table
- colored cards—red, yellow, green, blue, and other colors (optional)
- meterstick or yardstick
- people of different genders, eye colors, ages, athletic abilities, facial shapes, and some who wear glasses and some who do not

Your eyes are more than sensory organs that allow you to perceive light. There are cells in the eyes (cone cells) that respond to and differentiate among the various colors of light. There are also cells (rod cells), used primarily in dim light, that can detect only black and white.

When light strikes the retina, these cells respond by generating nerve impulses that travel along the optic nerve to the brain. The central part of the retina, the macula lutea, is rich in cone cells. As you know, the fovea centralis, where vision is clearest, contains only cone cells. This suggests that only cone cells are used when you read or look at the details of an object.

The outer, or peripheral, parts of the retina contain mostly or entirely rod cells. Rod cells contain a substance called rhodopsin, or visual purple.

Rhodopsin breaks down into two smaller molecules in the presence of light. In bright light, most of the rhodopsin is quickly decomposed. During dim light it is produced faster than it decomposes and so its concentration increases.

EYES IN DARKNESS

After spending an hour or more in sunlight or in a bright room, go into a dark or dimly lighted room. How well can you see? Sit quietly in the room for a few minutes. Can you see any better now? What evidence do you have that the amount of rhodopsin in the rod cells of your eyes has increased?

After a few minutes, try to look at an object in the dark room. Do you see it better by looking at it directly or by viewing it through the sides of your eyes? Can you see the color of objects in the dark room? What do your observations tell you about the differences between rod and cone cells?

When you are outside at night, look directly at a dim star. Then look at it from the side of your eye. From which position do you see it more clearly? Can you explain why?

EYES IN LIGHT

Peripheral vision is the ability to see objects that are to one side of you. In baseball, a good hitter must be able to keep the image of a fast-moving ball fixed on the centers of his or her retinas. A good basketball or hockey player, however, must always be aware of the position of his or her teammates so that accurate passes can be made. That person is often off to one side; consequently, the passer must have good peripheral vision. The player must be able to see from the "corners" of the eyes.

As you can see from Figure 5a, light that enters your eyes from the sides falls primarily on the periphery of your retina. What kind of light-sensitive cells are located in that region of the retina?

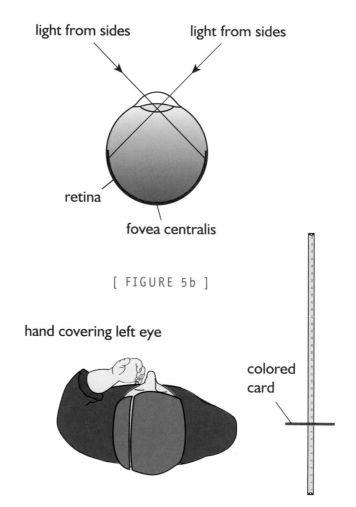

[FIGURE 5a]

light from sides   light from sides

retina

fovea centralis

[FIGURE 5b]

hand covering left eye

colored
card

5 a) Light from the side of your body must fall on the periphery of
your retina. What kind of receptor cells will respond to this light?
b) An overhead view of an experiment to test for peripheral
vision. A colored card is moved forward along a measuring stick
until the subject can see it.

You can determine the extent of your peripheral vision. Sit at a high table with your chin on your fist. Stare straight ahead at a mark or a small object that is about 2 m (6 ft) beyond the table.

Cover one eye while a friend slowly slides a colored card at eye level forward along a fixed measuring stick near your head, as shown in Figure 5b. Tell your friend when you first see the front edge of the card.

Record the position of the card on the measuring stick at that point. Then tell your friend when you can identify the card's color. Again, record the position of the card when you can first identify its color.

Repeat the experiment with cards of different bright colors—blue, green, red, and yellow, as well as black and white. Does the color of the card seem to affect the position at which you first see the card? Does the color of the card affect the position at which you can first identify color? If it does, which color is detected first? Which color is detected last?

Repeat the experiment with your other eye. Do both eyes seem to have the same peripheral vision? Now switch places and repeat the experiment to measure your friend's peripheral vision.

Try the experiment with a number of different people. Does peripheral vision seem to be related to a person's gender? Eye color? Age? Athletic ability? Facial shape?

Do eyeglasses help or hinder a person's peripheral vision?

Design and carry out an experiment to measure the upper and lower limits of a subject's visual field. Include measurements of the field over which your subjects can see color.

Build a sphere to show the visual field of the average person. On that same field, draw the smaller area to represent the field in which color can be seen.

IT'S WHERE THE EYES ARE

Suppose your eyes, like those of many animals, were on the sides of your head instead of in front. You would have a much wider field of vision.

You would be much better able to see things to your side and behind you. Frogs can sit in water with only their eyes above the surface and see in a complete circle of 360 degrees.

Unlike many animals, primates (including humans) and some other animals, such as bears and wolves, have both eyes on the front of their heads. Such a position reduces the animal's field of vision. Are there any advantages to having both eyes at the front rather than on opposite sides of the head? If there are, what are they?

Science Fair Project Ideas

- How can you use your data from Experiment 1.4 to determine the angle at which a subject can first see an object and the angle at which a subject can first see color?

- Design and carry out an experiment to determine whether the rod cells we use to view objects in dim light are more sensitive to light of a particular color.

Materials:

-bright, frosted lightbulb

-light-colored wall

-white paper

-ruler

-sheets of bright red, green, blue, white, and black construction paper; also (if possible) sheets of yellow, cyan (blue-green), and magenta (pinkish-purple)

-a dark room

-flashlight

-scissors

Stare at a bright, frosted bulb for a few seconds. Keep your eyes focused on the bulb; do not shift your gaze. Then turn away from the bright light and look at a light-colored wall. You will see a colored image of the bulb on the wall. Of course, there isn't any light there; it only seems to be there. The light you think you see is called an afterimage.

What is the initial color of the image? What happens to the color of the image as you watch it? Is the afterimage still present if you close your eyes? For how long does the afterimage persist?

Can you block out the afterimage by holding your hand in front of the afterimage you see on a wall, or does the image then appear on your hand? What does this tell you about the actual location of the afterimage?

Once the afterimage disappears, which will take more time than you think, repeat the experiment. This time hold a sheet of white paper in your hand. After viewing the afterimage on the wall, shift your gaze to the paper. What happens to the size of the afterimage if you again focus your eyes on the wall? What happens to the size of the afterimage as you shift your vision from far to near? From near to far? How might you explain the change in the size of the afterimage? Do you think the actual size of the image on your retina changes? What happens to the lens in your eye as you shift from near to far or far to near?

Allow time for your eyes to recover and the afterimage to disappear. Then stand close to the bright bulb and look at it again with only one eye open. Your other eye should be closed and covered with your hand because light can pass through your eyelid. Can you see an afterimage with the eye that was open? Can you see an afterimage with the eye that was closed? Based on the results of this experiment, does an afterimage form in the eye or in the brain? What makes you think so?

Allow time for your eye to recover and the afterimage to disappear. Then view the bright light out of the corner of one eye so that the image falls on the periphery of your retina, where there are only rod cells. Do you see an afterimage when the image of a lightbulb forms on the side of your retina? Can you explain the result of this experiment?

AFTERIMAGES OF COMPLEMENTARY COLORS

All the different colors of light can be obtained by mixing the three primary colors of light, which are red, green, and blue. For example, if you mix red and green light by shining both colored lights on the same area of a white wall, you will see yellow light. Mixing red and blue produces magenta (pinkish-purple). Cyan (bluish-green) can be obtained by mixing green and blue light. Mixing all three primary colored lights (red, green, and blue) will produce what you see as white light.

Two colored lights that produce white when mixed are said to be complementary colors of light. For example, red and cyan are complementary colors of light. When they are mixed, white light is seen. After all, cyan is a mixture of blue and green light, so when red light is added, the three primaries needed to produce white light are present. The color triangle in Figure 6 shows the primary colors of light at the vertexes with their complementary colors on the sides opposite the vertexes.

You can do an experiment to find the color of the afterimages you see after staring at a particular color. You will need to cut squares 5 cm (2 in) on a side from sheets of bright red, green, blue, and black construction paper. If possible, obtain yellow, cyan (blue-green), and magenta (pinkish-purple) squares as well.

Place a blue square on a sheet of white paper. Place a second sheet of white paper beside the one with the colored square. Stare at the colored

[FIGURE 6]

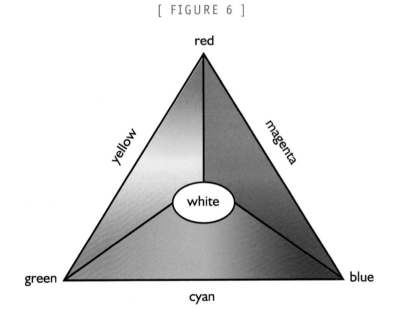

This color triangle for colored light shows the primary colors at the apexes and their complementary colors on the opposite sides. The colors along the sides show the color produced when the primary colors at each end of the side are mixed. White, at the center of the triangle, is the result of mixing all three primaries.

square for about thirty seconds. Then shift your eyes and stare at the blank sheet of white paper. What is the color of the afterimage you see?

Repeat the experiment with each of the other colored squares. What color are the afterimages of each of these squares?

Try the experiment with each of the colored squares again. As you stare at each of them, what do you notice about the edges of the squares?

Put a small red square on a larger blue square. Predict what the afterimage will look like if you stare at these squares for thirty seconds. Try it. Were you right?

What will be the colors of the afterimage that you will see when you stare at a small red square on a larger green square? A small blue square on a larger green square? A small green square on a larger magenta square? A small blue square on a larger yellow square? A small red square on a larger cyan square? A small black square on a larger white square?

Prepare colored squares, each about 3 cm (1.25 in) on a side, from pieces of red, blue, green, and white construction paper. Arrange the squares to form a larger square, as shown in Figure 7. Predict what you will see if you stare at the center of this multicolored square for 30 seconds and then turn your eyes onto a blank sheet of white paper beside the square. Try it! Was your prediction correct?

POSITIVE AFTERIMAGES

The afterimages you have seen so far in this experiment are negative afterimages similar to those produced on the film in a film camera. A bright white stimulus produces a black image. The image of the original bright object persists but the colors are opposite, or complementary, in the afterimage. Black objects produce white afterimages, white produce black, red produce cyan, and so on.

In positive afterimages, the afterimage is the same color as the object that produces it. To create a positive afterimage, go into a dark room and stay there until your eyes have adapted to darkness. This may take 10 minutes or more. You will find that with time you are able to see more

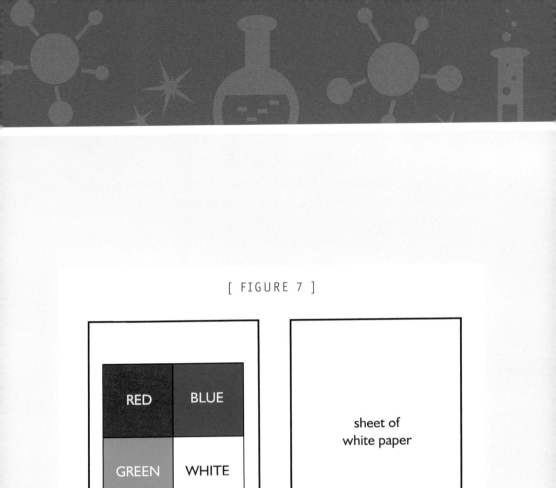

[FIGURE 7]

| RED | BLUE |
| GREEN | WHITE |

sheet of
white paper

For thirty seconds, stare at a multicolored square made of smaller red, blue, green, and white squares resting on a white background. Then shift your gaze to a sheet of white paper. Predict the colors you will see in the afterimage.

objects in the dark room. The rhodopsin pigment, or visual purple, in your rod cells is resynthesized after having been decomposed in bright light. As the concentration of rhodopsin in the rod cells rises, the capacity of your cells to respond to dim light increases.

Once your eyes have adapted to the dark, point a flashlight at your eyes. Turn the light on and look right at it for an instant and then turn it off. Turn your eyes toward a wall and you will see an afterimage. How does the afterimage compare with the light that caused it?

The light caused the rhodopsin in the rod cells to decompose. After the light was extinguished, the rhodopsin continued to break down, causing a positive afterimage.

After exposure to bright light, the rhodopsin quickly breaks down and we lose our ability to form positive afterimages. The rod cells, lacking rhodopsin, cannot respond. We are left with only cone-cell vision.

The chemicals in cone cells also break down, but they regenerate more rapidly than rhodopsin. To avoid cone-cell fatigue, we continually shift our eyes slightly so that the light in the images on the retina falls on different cone cells, giving previously stimulated cells time to recover.

Science Fair Project Idea

Using colored pencils or pens, draw a picture of a flag that will have the flag of the United States as its afterimage. Use your picture in an experiment.

CONE CELLS, COLOR VISION, AND AFTERIMAGES

Cone cells are located near the center of the retina directly behind the lens. They can detect color, but they do not respond to dim light. Only rod cells are stimulated by dim light, and rod cells can detect only shades of gray, not color.

According to one theory of vision, there are three types of cone cells, one for each of the primary colors of light—red, green, and blue. If light from a blue object enters our eyes, it is mostly the cone cells responsive to blue light that are stimulated. Similarly, green light stimulates primarily the cone cells sensitive to green light, and red light stimulates cone cells that respond to red light. Yellow light will excite both the red- and green-sensitive cone cells. Which cone cells, then, would be stimulated by a magenta-colored object? Which cells would respond to cyan?

Cone cells, like other sensory and muscle cells, become fatigued through use. When you look at something yellow, a combination of red and green light is reflected to your eyes. Consequently, the cone cells that respond to red and green light are the ones that tire with prolonged exposure. When you then turn your eyes to view a white background, the cone cells sensitive to blue light are the predominant ones to respond because they, unlike the cone cells responsive to green and red light, are not fatigued. The afterimage, therefore, appears to be blue.

Using a similar argument, explain why the afterimages produced after staring at cyan and magenta objects are red and green respectively.

Materials:
- straight edge, such as a yardstick
- blackboard or easel
- chalk or pen
- ruler
- as many people to serve as subjects as possible
- 2 thin sheets of white cardboard, each about 30 cm x 40 cm (12 in x 16 in)
- table

Figure 8a is sometimes known as the vertical-horizontal illusion, and Figure 8b is known as the Müller-Lyer illusion, named for the scientists who devised it. You can use these two illusions to test subjects in a quantitative way.

Using a straight edge, such as a yardstick, make a horizontal line about 30 cm (1 ft) long on a blackboard or easel. To begin the experiment, record your first subject's name, age, and gender. Then ask your subject to draw a vertical line upward from the center of the horizontal line until the vertical line, according to his or her estimate, is equal in length to the horizontal line. After the subject has drawn the vertical line, measure the line and record the estimate next to your subject's name in your science notebook.

Repeat this experiment with as many subjects as possible.

Müller-Lyer Illusions

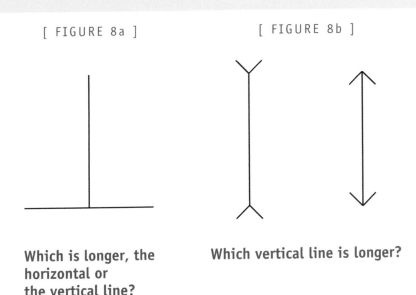

[FIGURE 8a]

Which is longer, the
horizontal or
the vertical line?

[FIGURE 8b]

Which vertical line is longer?

You can use the following illusions to test your subjects: a) the vertical-horizontal illusion and b) the Müller-Lyer illusion.

Do all your subjects underestimate the length of the vertical line they believe to be equal in length to the horizontal line? Does your data indicate that older people are better at estimating the vertical length than younger subjects? How about gender? Are girls and women better at making the estimate than boys and men?

The Müller-Lyer illusion can be tested in a quantitative way as well. On each of two thin sheets of white cardboard, draw a straight line along the center, using a heavy, dark pen. On one line place large arrowheads at each end. On the other draw an arrow tail at one end. Holding the cardboards on a tabletop as shown in Figure 9, slide the sheet with the arrow tail behind the sheet with the arrowhead. Start with the line that has arrowheads much longer than the line with the arrow tail. Move the tail sheet until the subject tells you the lines are

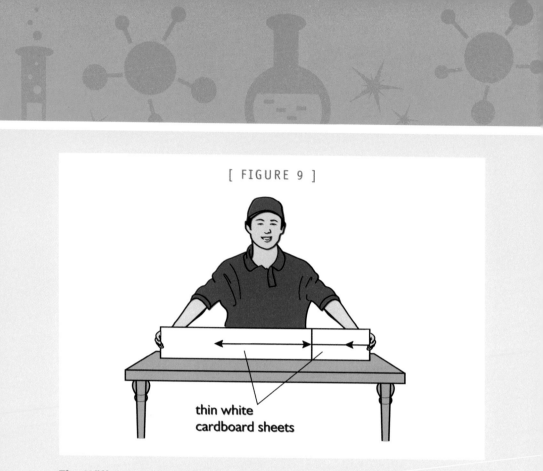

[FIGURE 9]

thin white
cardboard sheets

The Müller-Lyer illusion can be tested in a quantitative way using two sheets of cardboard and a tabletop, as shown.

of equal length. Then measure the length of the tailed line and record your data next to the subject's name.

Do all your subjects underestimate the length of one line they believe to be equal in length to the other line? Does your data indicate that older people are better at estimating equal lengths than younger subjects? How do girls and women compare to boys and men?

Chapter 2

The Sense of Hearing

YOUR EARS ARE THE ORGANS THAT ENABLE YOU TO HEAR. They allow you to perceive sounds in the world around you, locate the position of a singing bird, recognize the sound of a familiar voice, listen to a lecture, and respond to the warning sound of a horn. However, without the brain to which your ears are connected by the auditory nerve, you would hear nothing. For, ultimately, the sense of hearing is to be found not in your ears but in the lower sides (temporal lobes) of your brain. It is there that you make sense of the sounds that reach your ears.

Sounds are caused by vibrating objects. Their vibrations produce pulses of pressure that can travel through gases, liquids, or solids. Most of the sounds you hear are transported to your ears by air.

Air, like all gases, is made up of tiny particles called molecules. Most of the air (78 percent) consists of nitrogen molecules. There are also oxygen molecules (21 percent), and small amounts of other gases such as argon and carbon dioxide.

Sound that travels through air is produced when a vibrating object pushes air molecules closer together, creating a region of higher pressure. That region of higher pressure then pushes on molecules ahead of it until the pulse of higher pressure reaches your ear.

Of course, a vibrating object produces many of these regions of high pressure as it moves back and forth. Consequently, a series of high pressure regions (compressions) with lower pressure regions (rarefactions) between them travel outward through the air. A series of compressions and rarefactions traveling through a medium such as air is called a sound wave. A diagram of such a sound wave is shown in Figure 10.

These sound waves, unless blocked, spread outward in all directions from the vibrating object.

It is important to realize that although sound waves move through air, the molecules of air simply move back and forth. They transport the wave, but they do not move with it. You can see the same thing if you watch a cork on the surface of a still pond. If you make some water waves by dipping a stick up and down in the water, the waves travel outward from the stick. As they pass the cork, you see the cork bob up with each passing crest and down with each trough. However, the cork does not move with the water wave. It simply bobs up and down in place. The same is true when a wave created by humans raising their arms travels around a sports stadium. The fans remain in their position, but the wave they create by raising their arms vertically travels horizontally along the crowd.

Most sounds do not consist of a single pulse but of many pulses produced by a vibrating object and closely spaced in time. The vibrating object could be the string of a violin or cello, the oscillating air from a trumpet, the head of a drum, the motor of a car, or, more commonly, the vocal cords of another person. Humans usually communicate through spoken words, and the vibration of vocal cords gives rise to the sounds we call speech.

The distance between successive compressions, or rarefactions, in a sound wave constitutes a wavelength. The number of waves generated per second is the frequency of the waves. It is also, of course, the frequency of the vibrating object producing the sound.

Sound waves with a high frequency and a short wavelength are said to have a high pitch. Such sounds are made by someone singing soprano or striking the keys on the right-hand side of a piano. Sound waves with a low frequency and a long wavelength are said to have a low pitch.

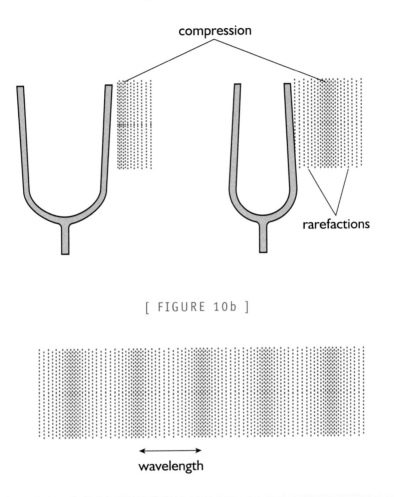

compression

rarefactions

wavelength

10 a) A vibrating object, such as a tuning fork, pushes air molecules together, producing a region of compressed air. Each compression is followed by a rarefaction (a region of low pressure) as the vibrating object moves in the opposite direction. b) A series of equally separated compressions and rarefactions traveling through air or another medium constitutes a sound wave. The distance between successive compressions or rarefactions is a wavelength.

Sounds such as those made by a bass singer, a bass fiddle, or the keys on the left-hand side of a piano have a low pitch.

When sound waves reach your ear, the changes in pressure that make up the waves cause your eardrum to move in and out with the same frequency as the sound. The changes in pressure needed to move your eardrum are very small. The human ear is incredibly sensitive. It can detect intensities as small as a trillionth of a watt per square meter. (That is less than the energy involved in a rustling leaf.) To understand what happens after a sound wave reaches your eardrum, you need to know the anatomy of the ear.

2.1 Your Pinnae and an Old-Fashioned Hearing Aid

Materials:
- radio
- large sheet of heavy paper, such as a poster

The flaps on either side of your head that you normally refer to as your ears are really only a part of your ears. Each of those flaps, consisting of skin, muscle, connective tissue, and cartilage that are attached to the sides of your head, are called *pinnae*. They are an important part of your organ of hearing. To see why, stand near a radio and either turn down the volume or stand far enough away so that you can barely hear the sound. Now face the radio and use your fingers to turn your pinnae toward the sound. What do you notice about the loudness of the sound when you do this?

A less direct way to see how your pinnae aid in hearing is to use an old-fashioned hearing aid. Long before battery-powered hearing aids, people who were hearing-impaired used a cone-shaped device that looked like a megaphone to help them hear better. You can make such a device by rolling a large sheet of heavy paper, such as a poster, into a conical shape. Hold the narrow end of the cone over one ear and turn that ear toward the radio you used before. Explain how the device improves your hearing.

Science Fair Project Ideas

- On the sidelines at professional football games you often see concave-shaped disks that resemble the "dishes" used to pick up satellite TV signals. TV crews use the devices to pick up sounds from the field. How do these devices work?
- If your school has an audio oscillator, use it to measure the range of frequencies that different people hear. Test people of different ages. What do you find? Does the volume at which you play the sounds have any effect on people's ability to hear the frequency? Is there a frequency range that everyone can hear? If so, what is it?

Materials:

-table fork or tuning fork

-wooden cutting board

-cotton

Tap the tines of a table fork or a tuning fork against a wooden cutting board. Hold the fork near one ear. Tap the tines against the board again, but this time hold the handle of the fork between your teeth. By doing so you provide a bony pathway from the fork to your ear. How does the sound compare with the one you heard when the sound waves were carried by air? Where does the sound seem to be coming from?

Put cotton in one ear and again place the handle of the vibrating fork between your teeth. In which ear does the sound seem to be louder? Can you explain why?

ANATOMY OF THE EAR AND TRANSMISSION OF SOUND WITHIN IT

The human ear has three parts—outer, middle, and inner (see Figure 11a). The pinna attached to the side of your head collects sound waves and reflects them to the tube that leads to the eardrum. Sometimes you may cup your hand around your pinna to capture more sound when you have trouble hearing something.

The tube within the pinna that leads to the eardrum is called the *external auditory canal*. The inner end of this tube is surrounded by the temporal bone of the skull. Sound waves travel along this canal until they strike the eardrum, or *tympanic membrane*, which they cause to vibrate. The tympanic membrane marks the inner edge of the external ear. It separates the outer ear from the middle ear.

The air-filled middle ear lies within the temporal bone. It has a volume of less than half a cubic centimeter and connects to the top of the throat by means of the *eustachian tube*. The eustachian tube provides a passage that allows the pressure on both sides of the eardrum to be equal. When you have a cold or an infection, the 3.6-cm-long eustachian tube

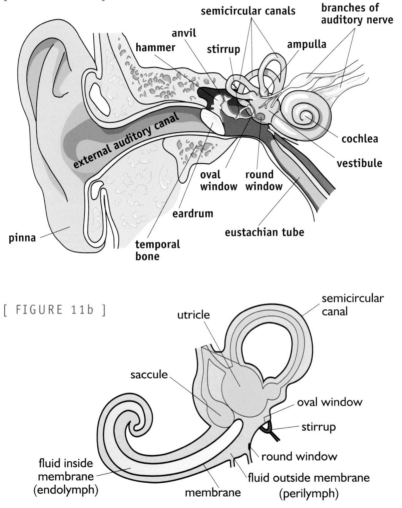

[FIGURE 11a]

semicircular canals

branches of
auditory nerve

anvil

hammer

stirrup

ampulla

external auditory canal

cochlea

vestibule

oval
window

round
window

eardrum

eustachian tube

pinna

temporal
bone

[FIGURE 11b]

semicircular
canal

utricle

saccule

oval window

stirrup

round window

fluid inside
membrane
(endolymph)

membrane

fluid outside membrane
(perilymph)

11 a) This diagram shows the outer, middle, and inner ear. The outer and
middle ear are separated by the eardrum. The middle and inner ear
are separated by the oval and round windows. b) The membranous
labyrinth encloses a fluid (endolymph) and is surrounded by a fluid
(perilymph) that separates the membrane from its bony surroundings.

may become blocked. This prevents equalization of pressure on both sides of the eardrum, causing reduced hearing until the tube is reopened.

Often, the tube will become obstructed with fluid in the pharynx (the region behind your tongue). Swallowing, yawning, or sneezing may clear the tube and equalize the pressure. If you have traveled by airplane, you may have had the experience of reduced hearing caused by unequal pressure between the outer and middle ear as the plane climbed to high altitudes or descended for a landing. Swallowing, yawning, or chewing gum may have opened the eustachian tube, allowing the pressure to equalize and your hearing to return to normal.

Within the middle ear are three bones—the hammer (*malleus*), the anvil (*incus*), and the stirrup (*stapes*). These three tiny bones form a series of levers that magnify the force on the eardrum about ten times. The hammer's handle is attached to the tympanic membrane. Its head is attached to the anvil. The anvil, in turn, is attached to the stirrup. The base of the stirrup rests on the oval window, or *fenestra vestibuli,* which separates the middle ear from the inner ear, or *labyrinth.*

The inner ear is a hollowed-out portion of the temporal bone. Within the labyrinth is a membrane, the *membranous labyrinth,* which encloses a fluid and which is itself encircled by another fluid that cushions the membrane from its bony surroundings, as shown in Figure 11b.

The membranous labyrinth consists of a *vestibule* with two small sacs, the *saccule* and the *utricle.* Behind the saccule and utricle are three *semicircular canals.* These appropriately named tubes lie at right angles to one another and are connected to the utricle. One end of each canal is enlarged to form what is called an *ampulla.* All these structures are filled with fluid and nerve endings that send impulses to your brain.

The coiled, snail-like *cochlea* lies in front of the vestibule. The *basilar membrane* stretches across the cochlea, dividing it into two parts. The upper side is separated from the middle ear by the oval window. The lower side is separated from the middle ear by the round window, or *fenestra cochlea.* Another membrane—the *vestibular membrane*—divides the upper side of the cochlea into two parts so that the cochlea contains three coiled channels.

2.3 A Look at an Eardrum and a Model Eardrum

Materials:

- a parent, sibling, or friend
- pen flashlight
- tin can
- can opener
- scissors
- large round balloon
- strong rubber band
- glue
- tiny mirror or a small piece of a broken mirror

Ask a parent, sibling, or friend to let you look into his or her ear. Gently pull on the pinna to straighten the external auditory canal as you shine a pen flashlight into the ear. At the inner end of the canal you may be able to see the eardrum. If your subject's auditory canal is very curved, you may not be able to see the eardrum. If that is the case, try looking into the ears of another subject whose ear canal is straighter.

To make a model of the eardrum, remove the top and bottom from a tin can. Use scissors to cut off the lower two thirds of a large balloon. Then stretch the bottom half of the balloon over one end of the can. Use a strong rubber band to hold the stretched balloon in place. Next, glue a tiny mirror or a small piece of a broken mirror to the balloon (see Figure 12a).

Once the glue has dried, find a place where you can reflect a small patch of light from the mirror onto a wall. Now let sound waves strike the model eardrum. You can do this by speaking into the can (see Figure 12b). How does the "eardrum" respond to loud as opposed to soft sounds? How does it respond to high-pitched as opposed to low-pitched sounds?

How is your model similar to a real eardrum? How is it different from a real eardrum?

FROM SOUND WAVES TO NERVE IMPULSES AND HEARING

When sound waves cause the stirrup to vibrate against the oval window, the fluid within the cochlea also vibrates. Thousands of hair cells of different lengths, together with supporting cells, are arranged along the basilar membrane. The length of the hair cells varies from about 0.13 mm to 0.28 mm. (A cross section of the cochlea showing the basilar membrane is seen in Figure 13.) The tectorial membrane lies above these hair cells. When sound waves are transferred to the fluid in the cochlea, the basilar membrane also vibrates. Certain hair cells respond to a given frequency by vibrating themselves. As they vibrate, they move against the tectorial membrane. The motion generates nerve impulses that travel to the brain where the sound is perceived.

Shorter hair cells vibrate in response to high-pitched sounds; the longer hair cells respond to sounds of low pitch. The vibration of the hair cells produces nerve impulses that travel to the brain, where the sound is perceived to be of a particular frequency and loudness.

Although our vocal cords can produce sounds ranging in frequency from only 85 to 1,100 hertz (Hz), human ears can detect sounds with a frequency as low as 20 Hz and as high as 20,000 Hz. (The hertz is the unit used to measure frequency. One hertz is equal to one vibration per second.) Humans, however, vary greatly in the range of sound frequencies they can hear. Generally, our ability to hear high frequencies decreases with age, and many older people have difficulty hearing sounds of low or high frequencies. Generally, people are most sensitive to sounds with frequencies of 2,000–3,000 Hz.

Other animals can hear sounds of much higher frequency. Dogs can hear frequencies as high as 50,000 Hz. That is why dogs respond to the high-pitched sounds of a whistle that we cannot hear.

Bats, which emit sounds with frequencies as high as 120,000 Hz, can hear sounds of the same frequency. In fact, they use these high-pitched sounds to detect the insects on which they feed. Sound waves produced by a bat are reflected from an insect's body. The fast-flying bat with its

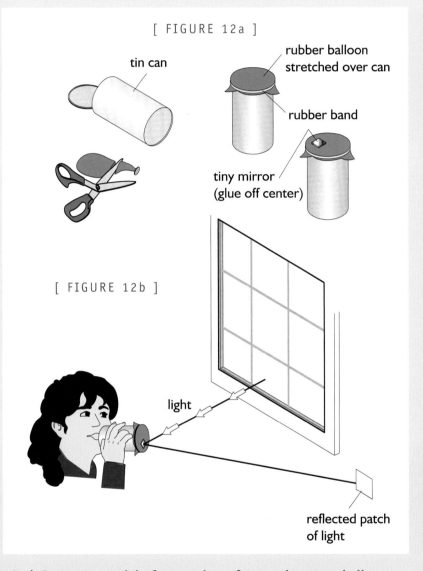

[FIGURE 12a]

tin can

rubber balloon
stretched over can

rubber band

tiny mirror
(glue off center)

[FIGURE 12b]

light

reflected patch
of light

12 a) Prepare a model of an eardrum from a tin can, a balloon, a rubber band, and a tiny mirror. b) Produce sound waves that strike the "eardrum." See the magnified effect of the sound waves on the eardrum by watching the reflected patch of light on a wall.

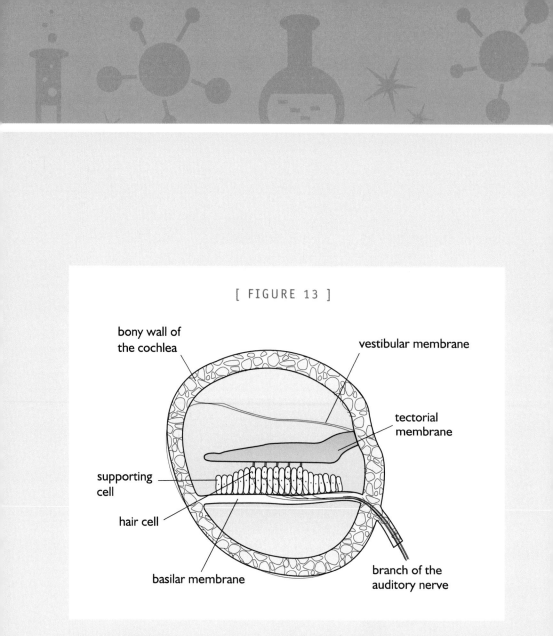

[FIGURE 13]

bony wall of
the cochlea

vestibular membrane

tectorial
membrane

supporting
cell

hair cell

basilar membrane

branch of the
auditory nerve

This cross-sectional view of the cochlea shows the basilar and tectorial membranes and the hair cells that connect to nerve cells from a branch of the auditory nerve.

large pinnae can sense these sounds and follow them to the prey on which it feeds.

Some animals, such as elephants and large whales (finback and blue), make sounds that we cannot hear because the frequencies of the sounds are less than 20 Hz. For the same reason, we cannot hear the lower frequencies of the sounds emitted by earthquakes and volcanoes, some of which are less than 1 hertz.

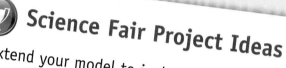

Science Fair Project Ideas

- Extend your model to include a model of the middle ear. Extend it still further by adding a model of the inner ear.
- Investigate how dolphins use the sounds they emit to detect their food and other objects in the sea.
- Over what distance can large whales hear the low-pitched sounds other whales emit?
- Are the organs of hearing found on the heads of all animals? If not, where else on the animals' bodies are they found?

THE INNER EAR AND BALANCE

The ampulla at the end of each semicircular canal contains a small organ known as the *crista ampullaris*. Rotation of the head in any direction, which may or may not be accompanied by rotation of the body, causes fluid in one or more of the semicircular canals to move. The movement of fluid pushes and bends hair cells that are embedded in the crista ampullaris. The hair cells then generate nerve impulses that travel to the cerebellum of the brain.

Materials:

- construction paper
- scissors
- ruler
- tape
- cardboard
- a friend
- piano
- musical instrument other than a piano (optional)

You have read that hair cells of different lengths on the basilar membrane of the cochlea respond to sounds of different pitch. The shorter hair cells respond to high-pitched sounds, and the longer hair cells, to sounds with lower pitch. This is known as the resonance theory of hearing.

Resonance has to do with the fact that objects that vibrate have a natural rate (frequency) of vibration. An object's natural rate of vibration is determined by its mass, stiffness, and size. If a force acts on a vibrating object at a frequency that matches its natural frequency, the size of the vibration will increase. This response to a natural rate of vibration is called resonance.

To demonstrate resonance and the effect of frequencies, prepare a series of paper rings. Using scissors, cut 2.5-cm- (1-in-) wide strips of differing lengths from construction paper. The longest one should be about 50 cm (20 in) long. (Long strips can be made by taping shorter strips together.) Other strips might be about 40 cm, 30 cm, and 15 cm (16 in, 12 in, and 6 in) long. Tape the ends of each strip together to make rings. Then tape the rings to a sheet of cardboard, as shown in Figure 14.

Shake the cardboard slowly back and forth from side to side at a very low but increasing frequency. The ring with the largest diameter will be the first to resonate. As you continue to increase the rate at which you move the cardboard back and forth, each ring, in turn, will resonate to

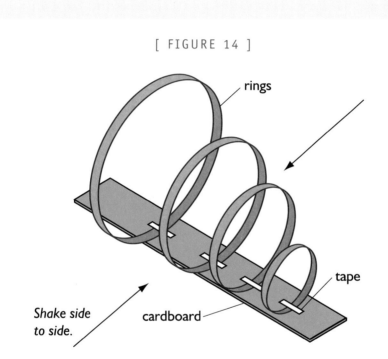

[FIGURE 14]

rings

tape

Shake side
to side.

cardboard

Resonating rings can be made from strips of construction paper that are taped to a sheet of cardboard.

a particular frequency. Will the rings also resonate to an up-and-down motion of the cardboard?

You can also demonstrate resonance using the strings of a piano. Ask a friend to push down on the right-hand pedal of a piano. If possible, look inside the piano when this is done. You will see that the dampers on all the strings are lifted when that pedal is down. Without dampers, all the strings are now free to vibrate. Sing a note into the piano or play a note on another instrument near the piano. Then listen to the piano. You will hear a sound from a piano string that is resonating in response to the pitch you sang or played. We say the piano string has been set into sympathetic vibration.

Use what you have learned in this experiment to explain why hair cells of different lengths on the basilar membrane respond to sounds of different frequencies. How might you explain our ability to detect differences in the loudness of a sound?

Science Fair Project Ideas

- Helen Keller, who became a well-known writer and speaker, was born both deaf and blind. How did she learn to communicate?
- Place open cardboard tubes of different lengths against your ear. How do the sounds you hear vary with the length of the tube? How are the sounds you hear related to resonance?
- You may have heard that if you place a conch shell against your ear you can hear the sea. What is it that you really hear?

2.5 The Doppler Effect

Materials:
- an adult driver and a car
- tape
- 9-volt buzzer
- plastic pail
- light rope
- a friend
- ripple tank, or a large, clear pan or box such as a glass baking dish or plastic sweater box at least 28 cm x 36 cm (11 in x 14 in)
- 2 chairs or tables
- ceiling light or lamp
- clear bulb with a straight-line filament (optional)
- water
- large sheet of white paper
- strips of soft cloth

Have you ever listened to the sound of a train's whistle or an automobile's horn as it approached you and then moved away from you? You may have noticed that the pitch of the sound rises as the vehicle approaches you and falls as the vehicle moves away from you.

Ask a parent or another adult to drive by you in a car. Ask them to sound the car's horn as they approach you and continue to sound the horn after they have moved past you. Ask them to repeat the experiment several times with the car moving at different speeds.

How does the pitch of the sound change as the car moves past you? How are the sounds you hear affected by the car's speed?

To examine this effect in a more controlled way, tape a 9-volt buzzer that produces a constant frequency of about 1,000 Hz to the bottom of an

light source

water tank

white paper

[FIGURE 15b]

15 a) A water tank rests on two chairs. It is illuminated by a
   light above the tank. Waves can be seen on the white paper
   screen on the floor beneath the tank. b) Dip your finger
   into the water at a constant rate to generate waves.

empty plastic pail. You can buy a buzzer in a radio or electronics store. Attach a light rope to the handle of the pail and ask a friend to swing the pail overhead while you listen to the sound some distance away. How does the sound you hear as the buzzer is approaching you differ from the sound you hear when the buzzer is moving away from you? Can you explain why the sounds differ? How does the speed at which the buzzer is moving affect the pitches you hear?

You can make a model of this effect (known as the Doppler effect) with a ripple tank or a large glass baking pan or a clear plastic sweater box. Support the clear container, which we will call a water tank, on two chairs or tables with a light directly over the pan, as shown in Figure 15a. A clear bulb with a straight-line filament turned so that its end acts as a point of light shining on the water tank works best, but an ordinary frosted bulb will do. To reduce unwanted reflected waves, cover the inside surfaces of the water tank's walls with pieces of soft cloth. Pour water into the tank to a depth of about 2 cm (1 in). Be sure the water tank is level so that the water is the same depth everywhere. Strips of paper placed under one end of the tank can be used to level it if necessary. Spread a large sheet of white paper on the floor beneath the tank.

Make waves by dipping your finger at a constant rate into the water in the center of the tank. As you can see, the circular waves spread outward and the wavelength is constant. Now, move your finger to one end of the tank and again make waves at a constant rate (see Figure 15b). But this time, as you make the waves, move your finger toward the opposite end of the tank. How does the wavelength of the waves in the direction your finger is moving compare with the wavelength of the waves in the opposite direction?

At which end of the tank will more waves arrive per second? In other words, at which end of the tank will the frequency of the waves be greater?

How does this experiment with waves in the water tank help to explain the Doppler effect?

Chapter 3

The Sense of Smell

HAVE YOU NOTICED THAT WHEREVER YOU GO, YOUR NOSE IS OUT IN FRONT LEADING THE WAY? What good is your nose, besides pointing you in the right direction or holding up a pair of glasses? Your nose helps you breathe and smell. This chapter is about the sense of smell—what goes on behind your nose, inside your head and brain.

Through your sense of smell, your brain is able to identify specific molecules floating in the air around you. Close your eyes, breathe deeply, and sniff the air. Do you smell a cup of coffee across the room, a peanut butter sandwich on the table, or someone's new perfume?

SCENTS: BIG BUSINESS AND NEW KNOWLEDGE

Industries around the world make products or use products to add, remove, control, and modify odors. Walk through a grocery store, and you will have a hard time finding a food or product that does not have a smell associated with it. Many products have odors added to them—from lemon-scented dishwashing liquid to scented candles. Some stores have displays of aromatic oils used in aromatherapy. Worldwide, perfume is a 15-billion-dollar industry! On the other hand, people spend billions of dollars on products that remove or control bad odors. They use everything from room deodorizers to body deodorants.

In recent years, our knowledge about odors and the sense of smell has grown. More than a thousand different genes in human DNA are used to make protein receptors that allow people to smell thousands of types of molecules. Scientists have learned a great deal about how the sense of smell works. They have identified many specific odor compounds produced by plants, animals, and humans, and they have learned how those compounds affect behavior. New methods of insect control use chemicals called pheromones that attract insects into traps. Other chemical odors are used to attract or repel fish, birds, and other animals.

Safety: If either you or a volunteer helping you suffers from allergies, migraine headaches triggered by odors, or asthma, do not use any foods or objects that can cause medical problems. Never smell hazardous products such as ammonia, bleach, gasoline, kerosene, or solvents. Do not breathe the fumes of other household products such as airplane glue, nail polish remover, or paint.

WHERE YOUR BRAIN MEETS THE WORLD OF SCENTS

When you breathe, air enters your nostrils and goes into two nasal passageways that lead up from the nose and then back down to the throat. Each nasal passage has thin bones called turbinates that direct the flow of air to the top of the nasal cavity. At the top of each nasal passage is a dime-sized spot called the olfactory epithelium. This spot is where your brain meets the world of scents. Here, special brain nerve cells called olfactory receptor neurons are directly exposed to the scents of the outside world. Molecules from the air touch these olfactory neurons and generate signals that the brain recognizes as specific odors.

The olfactory epithelium contains about 20 million olfactory receptor neurons (nerve cells). These millions of nerve cells are centered just below our eyes, behind the bridge of our nose (see Figure 16a). Each neuron has a highly branched end, called the dendrite, with many hairlike cilia. The dendrites are exposed to and detect odor molecules that dissolve in mucus around the cilia. A long portion of each neuron, called the axon, joins the axons of other olfactory receptor neurons to form olfactory nerves. These olfactory nerves go through the skull to connect with a brain structure called the olfactory bulb (see Figure 16b).

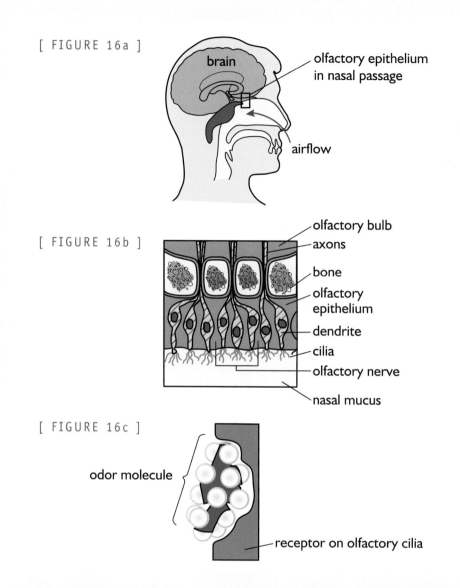

[FIGURE 16a]

brain

olfactory epithelium
in nasal passage

airflow

[FIGURE 16b]

olfactory bulb
axons
bone
olfactory
epithelium
dendrite
cilia
olfactory nerve
nasal mucus

[FIGURE 16c]

odor molecule

receptor on olfactory cilia

16 a) The olfactory epithelium is at the top of the nasal passages. b) The
olfactory epithelium is lined with special nerve cells whose branched
dendrite ends are covered with cilia and bathed with mucus. The long
axons of the olfactory receptor neurons extend through the skull into the
olfactory bulb. c) The tiny cilia contain olfactory protein receptor sites
into which selected odor molecules can fit and trigger electric impulses.
The olfactory bulb receives these nerve impulses, organizes them, and
allows the brain to interpret specific molecules as having unique odors.

Special protein molecules help bind odor molecules and concentrate the odor. Odor molecules from the air go into the thick, slimy mucus that coats the olfactory receptor neurons. Then the odor molecules bind at receptor sites along the cilia at the ends of the olfactory receptor neurons. Just as a key fits into a lock or a ball into a glove, odor molecules from the air fit into these special sites called olfactory receptors (see Figure 16c).

Although there are many millions of olfactory receptors in a person's olfactory epithelium, there are only about a thousand types of receptors. Each of the millions of olfactory neurons has just one type of receptor on it so there are also about a thousand types of neurons. A specific type of odor molecule will partially fit into only some of the receptors. All the neurons that have a partial fit with a certain type of odor molecule will send nerve signals along their axons to structures called glomeruli in the olfactory bulb. This unique pattern of signals from selected neurons is different from what would be generated by a different type of molecule. The brain interprets each signal pattern as a specific smell.

Where the world of scent touches the brain, people's lives are made richer. They are protected from danger by smelling smoke or spoiled food. They remember their past through the scent of flowers or a favorite perfume. They enjoy the aromas of cooking food and taste the flavor of food mostly through smell. The olfactory epithelium is continuously bathed in an incredible mixture of ever-changing molecules. As these molecules bind to receptor sites on olfactory neurons, electrical signals are sent to the olfactory bulb and brain. These signals are the smells of the world.

As you learn more about the sense of smell, you will learn about many different sciences. Understanding the sense of smell involves biology, chemistry, physics, medicine, human physiology, animal behavior, psychology, and more. This chapter investigates some of the basics of the sense of smell: how people identify, distinguish, and locate odors and how sensitivity to scents varies among people.

Materials:
- drinks in plastic bottles including Coke, Pepsi, Sprite, root beer, grape soda, Mountain Dew, and ginger ale
- 6 volunteers

Humans and animals have the ability to identify many foods by smell. This ability is important to the survival of many animals. In this experiment, you will explore how well people can identify some common soft drinks by smell alone.

Make a table (similar to Table 1) that lists the seven different drinks with enough columns for the drink identifications given by each of your volunteers. Have the first volunteer sit in a room. Show your subject the seven bottles that will be used. Ask the volunteer to close his or her eyes and keep them closed. Open the first bottle and hold it just beneath your volunteer's nose. Ask your subject to identify the smell and then close that bottle. Record the volunteer's choice (what he said it smelled like) beside that drink's name in your science notebook. Continue until all seven drinks have been tested. Do not present the drinks in any special order.

TABLE 1: Drink identification by smell

Drink	Volunteer 1 identifies	Volunteer 2 identifies	Volunteer 3 identifies
Coke			
Pepsi			
Sprite			
Root beer			
Grape soda			
Mountain Dew			
Ginger ale			

Repeat this experiment with additional volunteers. In your science notebook, record the answers from each volunteer. Make a new column of results for each volunteer.

When you have completed testing all the volunteers, compare their answers. How many items did each volunteer correctly identify? Were some of the drink odors more difficult to identify? What drinks were easier to identify?

When impulses from a unique odor with a distinct smell reach the brain, the brain easily distinguishes it. If the odor is one that the person commonly smells, the person has a strong memory of it and the odor is easy for the person to identify.

Humans may be able to distinguish (tell apart) up to 10,000 different odors. However, identifying a unique odor is more difficult than distinguishing between two odors. To identify a smell, you must know a name that goes with it and not just that it is different from another odor. Although people can distinguish between thousands of different smells, the average person can probably name and identify only a few hundred specific odors. However, some people, such as those who work preparing new perfume mixtures, have been trained to recognize thousands of different odors.

 ## Science Fair Project Idea

Try increasing the number of different drinks to smell. Add other noncarbonated drinks such as milk, orange juice, and different flavored sports drinks. Continue to try to determine which drinks are easiest to identify by smell and which ones are most difficult. Is it possible for your volunteers to distinguish different types of the same category drink—such as different brands of root beer or different brands of cola?

Materials:
- mustard
- piece of chocolate
- stick of cinnamon chewing gum
- 7 clean spoons
- partner

You probably know that people are able to recognize many specific foods or objects by using their sense of smell. But do you think people can distinguish between two or three different odors simultaneously?

First, you will need to prepare 7 different spoons with the items to be tested. Put similar amounts of each item in the spoons following these directions: spoon 1, chocolate; spoon 2, cinnamon gum; spoon 3, mustard; spoon 4, chocolate and cinnamon gum; spoon 5, chocolate and mustard; spoon 6, cinnamon gum and mustard; and spoon 7, chocolate, cinnamon gum, and mustard (see Figure 17). In spoons with two or three items, set the items side-by-side in the spoon. Do not cover one item with another.

Allow your partner to look at the spoons so he or she knows the possible combinations. However, keep the spoons far enough away so your partner cannot smell them.

Make a table (similar to Table 1) that lists the seven different spoons and what they contain with a column for the identification given by your partner. Have your partner close his or her eyes and keep them closed. Select one spoon and hold it under your partner's nose. Allow your subject to take just one quick sniff and then ask what the smell was. Repeat this procedure for all the spoons and be sure to record each answer in your table. Do not test the spoons in order from 1 to 7, but instead change the order around. Also, you can use the same spoon more than once and see whether the odors are identified the same way each time.

After you have finished testing your partner, trade places. Make another table for your identifications. Smell each spoon with your eyes closed. You may want to repeat the experiment several times.

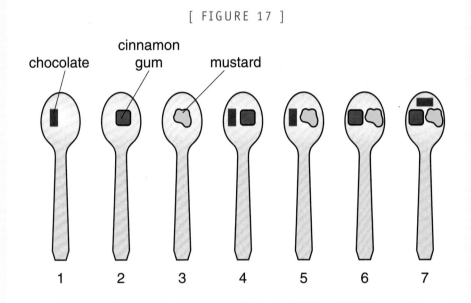

[FIGURE 17]

chocolate · cinnamon gum · mustard

1 2 3 4 5 6 7

Prepare spoons with odor samples containing the following: spoon 1, chocolate; spoon 2, cinnamon gum; spoon 3, mustard; spoon 4, chocolate and cinnamon gum; spoon 5, chocolate and mustard; spoon 6, cinnamon gum and mustard; and spoon 7, chocolate, cinnamon gum, and mustard.

You and your partner probably could identify the chocolate, cinnamon, and mustard easily when they were not mixed with anything else. Each of these items has a distinctive odor. When they were mixed two at a time, you still may have been able to identify the two items. However, people usually cannot pick out and identify three separate odors at the same time.

You know that you can look at a collection of things and identify many objects at once. Does it surprise you that your sense of smell is so different from your sense of vision? Can you think of ways that your sense of smell is more like vision or more like hearing?

Odors blend together like several notes played on a piano all at once. You can smell the blended odors just as you can hear blended music. A meal of different foods or even just one food item can consist of many different odor molecules blended together. However, just as you may be unable to separate out the individual notes in a song, you cannot identify all the unique odors in a complex mixture.

Olfactory receptor neurons have about a thousand different kinds of receptor sites (and millions of individual receptors) where specific parts of molecules fit and bind. A collection of one kind of molecule may fit into several specific types of sites and thus activate signals from several different types of receptors. Just like a combination of letters is used to make a word, a combination of activated receptors is used to identify a specific odor. However, because many different types of receptors could be activated, a person's brain cannot sort out and separate all the signals from several different types of molecules coming in all directions at once. People recognize the odor blend but cannot identify each unique odor.

Science Fair Project Ideas

- Try repeating this experiment but give your partner as long as he or she wants to try to identify the mixed odors. You may find that a person who has longer to concentrate can pick out first one odor and then the second and then the third. With continued sniffing, the brain may be able to distinguish each of three mixed odors but only by identifying them one at a time. Some professional perfumers have trained their sense of smell to sort out different odors from a complex mixture.

- Try using various combinations of foods and other smelly objects. Test as many different people as you can. Are some odor combinations more difficult to sort out because they smell so similar? Can you find other combinations of odors that are easier to distinguish?

Materials:

- an adult
- 5 empty glass jars
- tea bag
- water
- spoon
- microwave oven
- measuring container or separate cups with marks at 1/4, 1/2, 3/4, and 1 cup
- microwave-safe coffee mug
- 3 volunteers

Your nasal odor receptors and olfactory bulb may not be able to pick up the smell of a single molecule of limonene found in lemon juice. However, they could sense the odor of a whole bottle of lemon juice and many limonene molecules. Whether someone is able to smell an odor depends on how much of the odor is present and how many other odors are also in the air. In this experiment, you will test your volunteers' odor threshold for tea.

A *threshold* is the point at which a mental or physical effect begins to take place. In the sense of smell, the threshold is the number of odor molecules needed in the air for the odor to be detected. The absolute threshold is the smallest detectable amount of odor molecules. For example, humans are quite sensitive to the odor of sulfur-containing compounds. Hydrogen sulfide (H_2S) is a compound given off by rotten eggs and can be poisonous in excessive amounts. People can detect less than 1 gram of hydrogen sulfide even if it is mixed with 10 billion grams of air!

In this experiment, you will dissolve tea in water to reach the absolute threshold of the tea odor. In other words, you will find how much more water than tea there has to be before the smell of tea can no longer be detected.

To begin, **ask an adult** to place 1 cup of water in a microwave-safe coffee mug and heat it in a microwave oven for about 2 minutes. Be careful not to burn yourself; the water will be very hot. Put a tea bag in the coffee mug. Wait 3 minutes. Then remove the tea bag and stir the tea.

Measure 1/4 cup of tea and pour it into a clear jar. Then add 3/4 cup of water into the same jar. This is a 1/4 dilution of the original tea. In the remaining four jars you will be diluting the tea more and more.

To make the remaining dilutions, first pour 1/2 cup of the tea dilution out of the first jar and put it in the second jar. Now add 1/2 cup of water into the second jar. Take 1/2 cup of the mixture in the second jar and pour it into the third jar. Add 1/2 cup of water to the third jar. Now take 1/2 cup out of the third jar and pour it into the fourth jar. Then add 1/2 cup of water to the mixture in the fourth jar. Last, pour 1/2 cup from the fourth jar into the fifth jar and add 1/2 cup of water to the fifth jar. Pour 1/2 cup of the mixture in the fifth jar down the sink.

Now you should have the same amount of liquid in each jar. The color of the tea should get lighter as you go from the first to the fifth jar.

TABLE 2
Sample results of odor threshold detection

Jar	Tea dilution	Volunteer 1: Smelled tea?	Volunteer 2: Smelled tea?	Volunteer 3: Smelled tea?
1	1/4	Yes	Yes	Yes
2	1/8	Yes	Yes	Yes
3	1/16	Yes	Yes	Yes
4	1/32	No	Yes	No
5	1/64	No	No	No

The amount of the original tea in each jar is as follows: jar 1, 1/4; jar 2, 1/8; jar 3, 1/16; jar 4, 1/32; and jar 5, 1/64.

Make a table to record your observations (see Table 2). Have each volunteer first smell the tea in the coffee mug so he or she knows the aroma of tea. Then have your volunteer start with the first jar and move to the fifth, smell each jar, and say whether tea is smelled. Record your volunteer's answers. Repeat this process with each volunteer and, finally, smell each dilution yourself. Record the results in your table.

Did all of you have the same absolute threshold for tea odor? Did some people stop smelling tea at different dilutions than others? Could you see the tea even when you couldn't smell it?

🏆 Science Fair Project Ideas

- Repeat the experiment with people of all ages—children, teenagers, and adults. Does age affect odor threshold? The sense of smell often declines in adults over 70, but very young children have not had as much experience in identifying odors. Can you explain any differences you find?
- Repeat the experiment again, but smell the fifth jar first and then go toward the more concentrated solutions. Do the results change when you start with the most diluted solution and go to the most concentrated? When humans smell a strong odor, they become less sensitive to smaller amounts of the same odor. Starting with a weaker odor may allow a person to sense more diluted concentrations of tea than in the first experiment.
- Repeat the experiment again but smell the jars in a random order. Do the results change?

3.4 The Speed of Odor

Materials:
- ruler
- orange juice
- measuring cup
- aluminum foil
- watch with timer or stopwatch
- empty plastic 2-liter soda bottle
- a volunteer

The molecules in air are in constant, random motion. These molecules travel at speeds of hundreds of miles per hour. They bump into billions of other molecules every second. Because so many molecules are moving so fast, each molecule goes only a short distance before it hits another molecule. Every time one molecule hits another molecule, they both change directions. Imagine what happens when two moving billiard balls collide. Now imagine billions of such collisions happening every second. Molecules are like tiny billiard balls that are constantly moving.

In this experiment, you will investigate how long odor molecules need to fight their way through all these collisions to reach your nose. After the odor molecules reach your nose, they can be sniffed into your nasal cavity. Then the odor molecules reach your olfactory epithelium where they are detected.

Rinse out an empty plastic 2-liter soda bottle. Pour 1/2 cup of orange juice into the clean, empty bottle. Shape a piece of aluminum foil into a small cap that can be placed over the bottle to seal it shut. When not in use, keep the bottle covered with this aluminum foil cap.

Make a table (similar to Table 1) that lists the five distances (3, 6, 9, 12, and 15 cm) with columns for the time your volunteer takes to smell the orange juice. Have the volunteer hold a ruler vertical and next to his or her face so it measures the distance from the nostrils to the bottle. The volunteer should close his or her eyes after the ruler is in place. Swirl the orange juice around the bottle and remove the aluminum cap.

Immediately move the open bottle so its top is at the 3-cm mark on the ruler (see Figure 18) and say "start." Start the timer. Ask the volunteer to say "stop" when the smell of the orange juice is first detected. Stop the timer. Move the bottle away from your volunteer and cover the bottle top after each trial.

Repeat this procedure at distances of 6, 9, 12, and 15 cm. Repeat all five distances at least three times, but do them in a random order. Make sure the orange juice odor is gone prior to repeating each trial. Record all the times in your table. List the distance the molecules traveled from the bottle to your volunteer's nose. Record the times next to the distance traveled.

Average the times for each distance and make a plot of average time (*y*-axis) versus distance (*x*-axis). Do you find that your data points give a curve (see Figure 19) indicating that as distance increases, the time to diffuse also increases?

The spreading of a collection of molecules is called *diffusion*. The mixture of molecules that gives the odor of orange juice diffuses through the air from the top of the bottle to your volunteer's nose. Does it make sense that the farther the molecules have to go, the longer it takes them to get there?

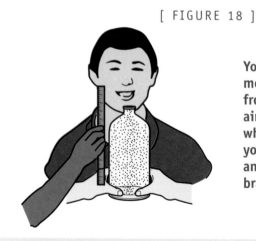

[FIGURE 18]

You can time how long molecules need to travel from a bottle through the air and into your nose where they finally reach your olfactory epithelium and are detected by your brain as a smell.

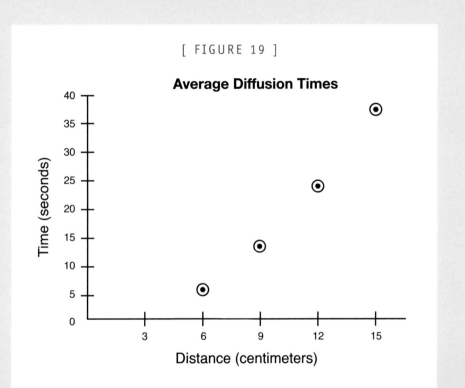

[FIGURE 19]

Average Diffusion Times

The graph shows the relation between the distance odor molecules have to travel to reach your nose and the time required for them to be detected as a smell.

Science Fair Project Ideas

- Repeat this experiment with different volunteers and compare the times people report to smell the odors. Are the numbers the same from one person to another or are some people's times shorter? Some people may be more sensitive to the odor (have a lower odor threshold) and report the smell more quickly.

- Repeat this experiment with different liquids. Smaller odor molecules diffuse more quickly. Can you tell any difference in the average diffusion times for different liquids?

- Hold the bottle about 30 cm (12 in) from your volunteer's nose and quickly squeeze the bottle so the walls are partly flattened. How quickly can you send odor molecules to someone's nose when you squeeze the bottle? How far can you send odor molecules with this method? Design an experiment to find out.

Materials:
- 2 rubber (latex) balloons
- plastic funnel
- tablespoon measure
- vanilla extract
- vinegar
- watch

Odor molecules must travel through the air to reach your nose before you can detect a smell. Then the odor molecules must pass through your nasal passages and dissolve in the mucus covering your olfactory epithelium. Finally the molecules must reach olfactory receptors into which they can fit. However, you would not smell anything unless odor molecules could first travel through the air. Do you think odor molecules can pass through a solid the same way they pass through the air?

To begin the experiment, first smell some vinegar. Next, pour a tablespoon of vinegar through a funnel into a balloon. Do not spill any liquid on the outside of the balloon. Blow up the balloon and tie it closed. Rinse off and dry the funnel and the tablespoon measure.

Vinegar is made of acetic acid molecules dissolved in water. When you detect the odor of vinegar, you smell acetic acid molecules. The acetic acid molecules found in vinegar have a pungent, or sharp, odor.

Smell vanilla extract. Now, pour a tablespoon of vanilla extract through the funnel into a second balloon and tie the balloon closed.

Vanilla extract is made of vanillin molecules dissolved in an alcohol and water mixture. When you detect the odor of vanilla extract, you smell vanillin molecules. Most people recognize the smell of vanillin because it is used in many foods and is associated with vanilla flavor.

Shake each balloon for about 60 seconds. Now, smell the outside of each balloon. Do you smell vanillin on the outside of the vanilla extract balloon? Do you smell acetic acid on the outside of the vinegar balloon?

Water is a polar molecule, meaning that it has a part that is more positive and a part that is more negative (see Figure 20a). The balloon

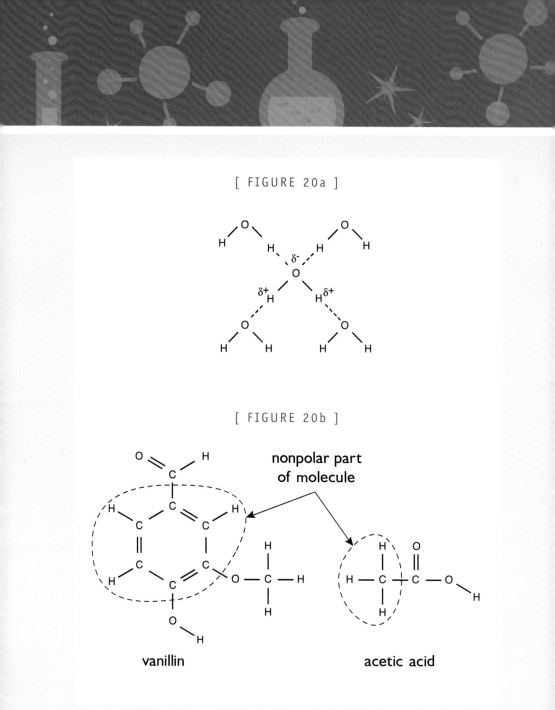

[FIGURE 20a]

[FIGURE 20b]

nonpolar part
of molecule

vanillin

acetic acid

20 a) Water molecules have a partial negative part (δ-) and partial
positive part (δ+) and are attracted to each other through a force
called hydrogen bonding. b) The vanillin molecule has a nonpolar
portion that helps it dissolve in rubber better than the smaller
acetic acid molecule, which tends to stay in water.

is made of rubber (latex) molecules. They do not have a more positive or negative part, so they are nonpolar molecules.

The acetic acid in vinegar is a polar molecule. It dissolves well in water but not in rubber. Vanillin is not as polar as acetic acid, so it does not dissolve as well in water. However, vanillin can dissolve in rubber better because it has a larger nonpolar part than acetic acid (see Figure 20b). Acetic acid moves through the balloon more slowly than vanillin.

 Science Fair Project Ideas

- Repeat the experiment using a mixture of vinegar and vanilla extract inside the same balloon. Vanillin and acetic acid pass through rubber at different speeds and have different odor thresholds. Can you use these differences to separate one odor from the odor mixture? Vanillin has a lower odor threshold than acetic acid so that you can detect much smaller amounts of vanillin. This difference in odor threshold makes it more complicated to say how many molecules have moved through the balloon. However, even though you can detect less vanillin, it still moves through the rubber balloon faster than acetic acid. Both its higher speed passing through the rubber and its lower odor threshold mean you will smell vanillin first on the outside of the balloon.
- Try other molecules such as peppermint extract or limonene. Limonene (a nonpolar molecule) is found in the oily liquid that can be squeezed out of an orange peel. Which odor molecules pass through a rubber balloon more quickly?

Chapter 4

The Sense of Taste

YOUR SENSE OF TASTE ARISES THROUGH TASTE BUDS EMBEDDED IN THE SURFACE OF YOUR TONGUE (Figure 21). In a taste bud, elongated cells with hairlike projections on their upper ends rest on supporting cells. Dissolved substances react with the hairs atop the taste receptor cells to produce nerve impulses that travel to the brain. It is within the brain that we perceive taste.

The nerve fibers from taste buds join the seventh and ninth cranial nerves before going to the brain. The tongue is also connected to the brain by fibers from the fifth, seventh, and twelfth cranial nerves.

Eating would be a rather dull affair were it not for our senses of taste and smell. As you probably already know from personal experience, smell and taste are closely linked to each other. But although smell and taste are closely related, there are differences between them. For a substance to be smelled, it must be a gas. For a substance to be tasted, it must be a liquid or be dissolved in a liquid.

There are only four basic taste sensations—sweet, salty, sour, and bitter. Other sensations that we call taste are actually combinations of the four basic tastes with one another and with sensations associated with smell. We will begin by investigating whether your sense of smell influences what you taste.

[FIGURE 21]

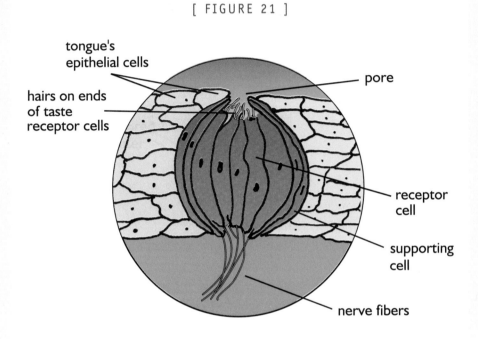

tongue's
epithelial cells

pore

hairs on ends
of taste
receptor cells

receptor
cell

supporting
cell

nerve fibers

The surface of the tongue contains many taste buds, elongated cells
with hairlike projections on their upper ends, as shown here.

4.1 A Tasty Smell

Materials:
-drinks in plastic bottles including lemon-lime soda, root beer, grape soda, and cola
-several volunteers
-straws
-cups

Is the flavor of a food or drink due to smell or taste or both? In this experiment you will investigate whether the smell of one soda can cause a person to "taste" that soda while drinking a different one.

Have a partner sit with eyes closed. Hold a freshly opened bottle of root beer just below the nose. Then hand your partner a straw that is placed in a bottle of lemon-lime soda farther from the nose (see Figure 22). Have your partner take one sip of lemon-lime soda. Ask what type of soda was tasted.

Wait a minute and repeat this activity with the next drink. Allow your subject to smell grape soda while taking one sip of lemon-lime soda. Wait a minute and then have him or her smell cola while taking a sip of lemon-lime soda. After each taste test, record what your volunteer smelled, what soda was actually given, and what was reported.

Lemon-lime soda has a sweet taste, but the aroma of the other drinks may dominate and make your partner think that the tasted drink was actually the smelled drink. What a person "tastes" is mostly due to what he or she smells. Did your partner report drinking lemon-lime soda or what was smelled? Repeat with additional volunteers (and fresh straws and sodas).

[FIGURE 22]

What do you taste if you sip one drink while smelling another?

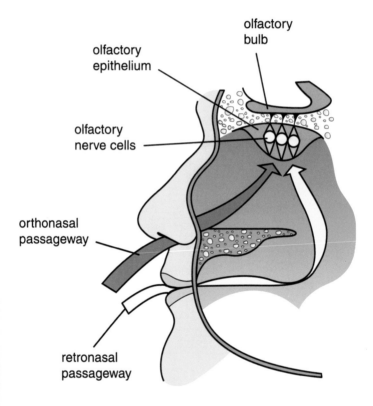

[FIGURE 23]

olfactory bulb

olfactory epithelium

olfactory nerve cells

orthonasal passageway

retronasal passageway

The olfactory epithelium is the spot where odor molecules are detected. Odor molecules can reach the olfactory epithelium through the nose (orthonasal passageway) or from the mouth through the back of the throat (retronasal passageway).

Molecules can reach the olfactory epithelium through the nose (orthonasal passageway) or from the mouth through the back of the throat (retronasal passageway, see Figure 23). When eating or drinking, odors traveling through the retronasal passageway usually dominate over odors traveling directly through the nose. However, in this experiment, if enough odor molecules go through the nose, then that scent may overwhelm the odor of what is in the mouth. In this case what you smell may also be what you "taste."

 ## Science Fair Project Idea

Prepare five mixtures of cups of Sprite and grape soda in the following amounts: 1 and 0, 3/4 and 1/4, 1/2 and 1/2, 1/4 and 3/4, and 0 and 1. Ask volunteers to identify each drink. Do not tell your volunteers what has been mixed together. Which drinks do they identify as Sprite and which as grape soda? Are they able to tell which is a mixture? Does the odor of one drink dominate the odor of the other?

⚑ 4.2 Taste Threshold

Materials:
- 7 drinking glasses
- cola
- water
- 7 spoons
- liquid measuring cup
- 4 volunteers
- 56 small disposable paper cups

In Chapter 3, you investigated odor thresholds and learned that a threshold is the minimum amount needed to detect the presence of something. In this experiment, you will investigate taste thresholds. When you taste a cola drink, you are detecting a complicated mixture of tastes and odors. The object of this experiment is to find the taste threshold for cola dissolved in water.

Add 1/2 cup of cola and 1/2 cup of water to a glass and stir. This glass is a 1/2 dilution of the original cola. Pour 1/2 cup of the cola from the first glass and 1/2 cup of water into a second glass and stir. Use a new spoon for each glass. Pour 1/2 cup of the cola from the second glass and 1/2 cup of water into a third glass and stir. Pour 1/2 cup of the cola from the third glass and 1/2 cup of water into a fourth glass and stir. Pour 1/2 cup of the cola from the fourth glass and 1/2 cup of water into a fifth glass and stir. Pour 1/2 cup of the cola from the fifth glass and 1/2 cup of water into a sixth glass and stir. Finally, pour 1/2 cup of cola from the sixth glass and 1/2 cup of water into a seventh glass and stir.

You should have 1/2 cup of diluted cola in glasses one through six and one cup in glass seven. The cola color should get lighter as you go from the first to seventh glass. From first through seventh, the glasses contain the following dilutions of the original cola: 1/2, 1/4, 1/8, 1/16, 1/32, 1/64, and 1/128.

In your science notebook, set up a table to record your observations (see Table 3). Pour a small amount of cola from each glass into seven paper cups. Have a volunteer taste the cola in each cup starting with the seventh and going to the first. After the volunteer sips the drink in each cup, ask what is tasted. Using fresh cups, repeat this process with other volunteers. Later, using fresh cups, have the same volunteers do this activity in reverse order, from the first to the seventh cup. Record all the results in your table.

TABLE 3

Sample results of taste threshold detection

Glass	Cola dilution	Volunteer 1 tasted	Volunteer 2 tasted	Volunteer 3 tasted	Volunteer 4 tasted
1	1/2	cola	cola	cola	cola
2	1/4	cola	cola	cola	cola
3	1/8	cola	cola	cola	cola
4	1/16	cola	cola	cola	water
5	1/32	water	water	cola	water
6	1/64	water	water	water	water
7	1/128	water	water	water	water

What was the least amount of cola your volunteers could taste? Did different people have different taste thresholds? Did it make a difference if the cola dilutions were presented from strongest to weakest or from weakest to strongest? Could you see color from the cola when it could not be tasted?

Science Fair Project Ideas

- Add 5 teaspoons of sugar to exactly 1 cup of water. Stir until all the sugar is dissolved. This sugar solution has about the same sugar concentration as a typical cola drink. Use this sugar solution in place of the starting cola drink and do the same seven dilutions. Repeat the original experiment using this sugar water. How do the results compare to the original cola taste test?

- Get a bottle of plain (no flavor) seltzer water. Seltzer water, also called carbonated water, is water that has had carbon dioxide gas dissolved in it under pressure. Carbonated water tastes different from regular water due to the dissolved carbon dioxide. Use seltzer water in place of the cola drink and do the same seven dilutions. Repeat the original experiment using these dilutions. How do the results compare to the original cola taste test?

4.3 Jellybean Taste Test

Safety: Some jelly beans contain peanut products. If anyone participating in this experiment is allergic to peanuts, check the ingredients in the jellybeans before use.

As earlier experiments demonstrated, the human brain interprets the sensation of flavor using two senses, smell and taste. Without each one the signal to the brain is not complete. In this experiment you will test the effectiveness of smell and taste working alone and together.

Separate the jellybeans into three flavors. Make sure the jellybeans are actually different flavors and not just different colors. The flavors should be listed on the package. Fill three resealable plastic bags, each with a different flavor of jellybean. Use only half of the jellybeans. These will be the taste bags. Then fill the remaining three bags, each with a different flavor. These will be the odor bags. In each odor bag, squeeze about half of the jellybeans (see Figure 24). This action will release odor molecules and make the jellybeans easier to smell.

Tell your first volunteer the three jellybean flavors you have chosen to use in this experiment. Now have your volunteer close his or her eyes. Let your volunteer smell each odor bag of jellybeans one at a time. After smelling each bag, ask your volunteer to identify the flavor. Prohibit guessing. Volunteers who cannot recognize the flavor should say they don't know. Record how your volunteer identifies each jellybean flavor.

Have your volunteer keep the eyes closed and hold his or her nose. In no particular order, offer a jellybean from each of the taste bags. After your volunteer takes a bite of a jellybean, ask for an identification of the flavor. Record the answer. After tasting each jellybean let your volunteer take a drink of water to wash the taste out of the mouth.

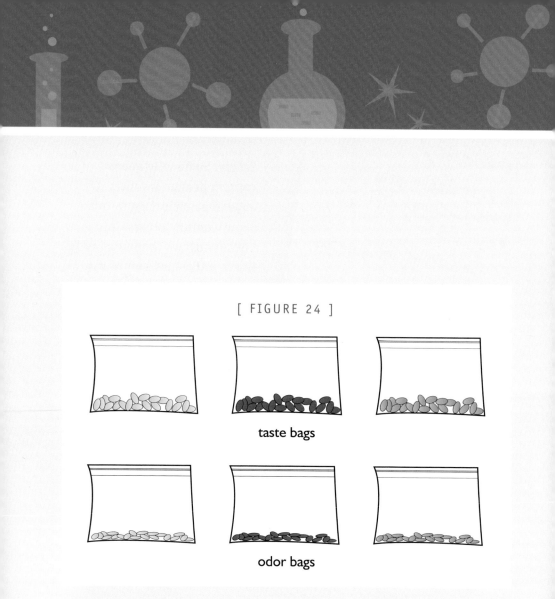

[FIGURE 24]

taste bags

odor bags

To compare taste and smell, make taste bags and odor bags for the three flavors of jellybeans.

For the last stage of the experiment tell your volunteer to keep eyes closed, but to let go of the nose. Once again offer each flavor of jellybean to taste one at a time. Record the identification of each flavor. Then repeat the experiment with your second volunteer and record the answers. Do this experiment with more people if possible.

Look at your results. Do you see any patterns? Can people identify the most flavors using their sense of smell, their sense of taste, or their senses of smell and taste together? Could some people identify flavors that others couldn't? How important was smell in determining flavor?

Everyone's taste and smell receptors are slightly different. These differences result from each person's unique body chemistry, genes, and psychology. Each person may experience the same flavor in a slightly different way. For this reason some people may have an easier time identifying flavors. Even though one smell or taste by itself may not be identifiable, together odors and tastes reinforce one another, giving the complete sensation of flavor.

 Science Fair Project Idea

Try giving volunteers marshmallows to eat while the volunteers smell a jellybean. Ask what is tasted. Does the smell of the jellybean affect the flavor of the marshmallow? Repeat this experiment with different jellybean flavors.

Materials:

-an adult

-ruler

-apple, potato, pear, cucumber, turnip, and onion (cut into cubes, 1 cm on a side)

-knife

-blindfold

-a friend

-toothpicks

-several people of different ages and genders

We sometimes enjoy the texture of food as well as its flavor. For example, most people prefer to bite into a crisp apple rather than a mealy one. How are taste, texture, and smell related? Can similar textures disguise the identity of a food? This experiment will help you to find out.

With the help of an adult, cut some cubes, 1 cm (0.4 in) on a side, from an apple, a potato, a pear, a cucumber, a turnip, and an onion. Then blindfold a friend who has not seen the food.

Ask your blindfolded friend to hold his or her nose tightly throughout the first part of this experiment. As you have seen, closing the nose will greatly reduce your friend's ability to smell the food. Using a toothpick, place one of the small pieces of food on your friend's tongue. Ask your subject to chew the food and try to identify both the taste and the food. Record the response as well as the actual food being tested. Repeat the experiment with each type of food and record responses and the food being tested in each case.

Next, repeat the experiment with each type of food, but this time have your blindfolded friend chew the small pieces of food with the nose open. Again, record responses and the actual food being tested in each trial.

Does adding the sense of smell help your friend identify the food? Does similarity in texture prevent identification of a food when the nose is closed? Does similarity in texture prevent your friend from identifying a food when the nose is open?

Try the experiment with a number of people of different ages and genders. Are older people less able to identify a food than younger people? Does gender make any difference? Do you have any evidence that some people have a stronger sense of smell than others? Do you have any evidence that some people are better able to distinguish foods by texture than others?

Chapter 5

The Sense of Touch

ALL OF OUR CONSCIOUS SENSES CONSIST OF RECEPTOR CELLS THAT RESPOND TO STIMULI BY GENERATING NERVE IMPULSES. These impulses are carried by nerve cells to a center in the brain where the impulses are interpreted. It is through our senses that we know what is happening within and outside our bodies.

Cells that respond to light, sound, and the chemical substances that we taste or smell are all located at specific sites in our heads. However, the cells that respond to touch, pain, pressure, and temperature are located in the skin and are spread over most of the body.

Some of the sensations we perceive lead to muscular action. We touch a hot stove and quickly pull our fingers away. We hear a warning and duck. Other sensations, the sounds found in a beautiful piece of music, for example, may elicit pleasant thoughts or memories but no physical response.

Although all sensations are perceived in the brain, we project these sensations to something outside the body or to some part of our body other than our brain. Those sensations that are projected externally include sights, sounds, tastes, smells, touch, temperature, and pressure. Sensations projected internally include pain, balance, hunger, thirst, nausea, fatigue, and a variety of muscular sensations.

Your skin contains receptors that respond to temperature, touch, pressure, and pain. The distribution of these receptors is not even. Some parts of the skin are very sensitive to touch; others are not. Parts of the body most exposed to injury are rich in pain receptors. Strangely, the brain, where pain is perceived, has no pain receptors.

Usually, we can accurately locate pain that arises from injury to the skin, but pain arising in internal organs is often more diffuse. A toothache, for example, may involve the entire side of the face and not just the bad tooth. Pains arising in the heart may seem to be located under the shoulder blades, in the muscles of the chest, or in the left shoulder and arm.

PERCEPTION

At this moment you are probably being bombarded by stimuli—light from all the objects around you; sounds of voices, birds, or cars; and tastes, if you are eating. You smell odors, possibly of food, perfume, soap, or newly cut grass. You receive touch sensations from this book, the chair on which you sit, and the floor that presses against your feet. Despite all these stimuli, you are generally aware of only a few. If you are listening to music, you tend to ignore other stimuli. Your attention is on the sounds. You may even close your eyes to reduce light stimuli. If you are looking at a beautiful painting, light stimuli prevail; you may be unaware of the words spoken by those nearby.

You perceive something when you become consciously aware of it by using one or more of your senses to receive stimuli from it. It might be a sentence you are reading, a musical theme you are hearing, or the odor of a flower you are smelling.

The knowledge you acquire through your senses is called perception. However, what you perceive is influenced by past experience. Furthermore, what you perceive may not be what it appears to be. The real world is often very different from the world you perceive.

5.1 One Touch or Two?

Materials:
- straight pins
- cardboard about 12 cm x 5 cm (4.5 in x 2 in)
- ruler
- a friend
- pencil
- several people

Your skin contains receptors that respond to touch. On some parts of the body, these receptor cells are packed closely together. In other areas of the skin they are farther apart.

The simple device shown in Figure 25 can be used to determine the separation between touch-sensitive cells. Push two straight pins into one side of a piece of cardboard about 12 cm (4.5 in) long and 5 cm (2 in) wide, as shown. Set the heads of the pins about 0.5 cm (0.25 in) apart. Set another set of pins about 1 cm (0.5 in) apart. Set a third set of pins about 2 cm (1.0 in) apart.

Ask a friend to close his or her eyes. Touch the two pins that are closest together gently against the tip on one of your friend's index fingers. Does your friend feel one or two points touching the skin? How close together are the touch receptors on the fingertip?

When you investigate the distance between touch receptors on other parts of the body, be sure you touch areas of the skin that are hairless. To see why, use a pencil to gently push a single hair on your arm. Can you sense that it has been touched? Many hairs have touch receptors near their roots beneath the skin. Can you find any hairs that do not stimulate touch receptors when moved?

Now, again with the pins 0.5 cm (0.25 in) apart, repeat the experiment on other places on the skin. Record your findings in your science notebook. **Do not put the pins near anyone's eyes.** You can try other fingertips, the palm of the hand, the back of the hand, different parts of the arm, the lips, ears, and neck, the calf and shin, and the back. Touch the pins to the skin in several places in each area you test.

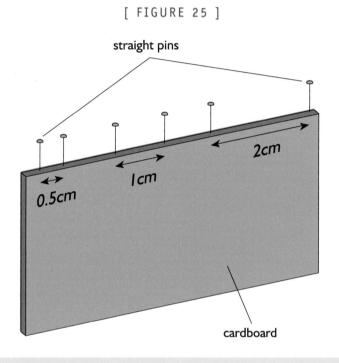

[FIGURE 25]

straight pins

0.5cm

1cm

2cm

cardboard

This simple device, made with cardboard and pins, can be used to test for single or multiple touch sensations.

Next, repeat the tests using the two pins that are 1.0 cm (0.5 in) apart. Can your friend now detect two touch points in regions that were reported as a single point before?

Try the experiment once more with the pinheads 2.0 cm (1.0 in) apart. Can your friend now detect two touch points in regions that were reported as a single point before?

If possible, carry out the experiment with a number of different people. Which parts of the body's skin appear to have the greatest number of touch receptors per area? Which parts have the fewest?

⟊ 5.2 Locating Touch

Materials:

- 2 felt-tipped pens of different colors
- a friend
- ballpoint pen
- ruler
- cotton swab
- cork
- pencil

How well can you locate a point on your skin where you have been touched? To find out, use a felt-tipped pen to mark points on a friend's fingertip, palm, wrist, arm, ear, neck, shin, and calf. Ask your friend to close his or her eyes and hold another felt-tipped pen of a different color in the dominant hand with fingers close to the tip. By holding the pen close to the tip, your friend will minimize any errors resulting from the angle at which the pen is held.

Use a ballpoint pen to touch, in turn, each of the colored marks you made before. Immediately after you touch the marked point, have your friend, with eyes still closed, try to mark the point you have just touched with the colored pen. Measure the separation between the two points. Repeat the experiment at least five times to obtain good indications of average error for each location.

Does the location of the touch point on the body affect your friend's ability to identify the point?

How can you measure the average error your friend makes in locating the touch points you established on different parts of the body? Is the average error in locating a touch point related to the ability to recognize two touch points instead of one, as was done in the previous experiment?

IT'S A MATTER OF WHERE YOU TOUCH

Pull a few fibers from a cotton swab. Gently drag the fibers across your palm and fingertips. Can you feel anything? Now draw the same fibers gently across your forehead, chin, face, nose, and ear. Can you feel anything in any of these places? What can you conclude?

Can you feel the cotton fibers if you drag them gently along the hairs of your forearm or leg? What can you conclude?

RECEPTOR FATIGUE

Touch receptors, like other receptors, become fatigued through use. Your brain is able to "filter" sensory information and ignore sensory impulses that are not essential to your well-being. As a result, you may become unaware of a touch sensation after a while. To experience this effect, extend your arm with the palm of your hand turned up. Place a cork on the inside of your forearm. How much time passes before you can no longer feel its presence? Does receptor fatigue take longer if the object is heavier?

PRESSURE

Touch your forearm with the eraser end of a pencil. Then gradually press harder with the pencil. As you press harder, you stimulate receptors deeper in the skin. These receptors respond to pressure. Pressure receptors are the cells that are stimulated when you place a heavy weight on your hand or arm. They enable you to detect the difference between light and heavy objects. Light objects stimulate touch receptors; heavy objects stimulate pressure receptors. When someone steps on your toe, both pressure and pain receptors are stimulated.

Science Fair Project Idea

Carry out an investigation to find out how people who are blind use their sense of touch to read.

Materials:
- fine-tipped felt pen
- ruler
- broom bristle
- a friend

In this experiment you will look more closely at the location of touch receptors. Use a fine-tipped felt pen and a ruler to draw grids, like the one shown in Figure 26, at different places on the skin of a friend. You might draw them on the inside of the lower forearm, back of the hand, thumb, palm, cheek, calf,

shin, and back. (If hairs are present on any of the skin areas you plan to test, shave them before you draw a grid. **Consult an adult about shaving skin.**) If the area is small, as on a thumb, use part of the grid. Draw similar grids in your science notebook for each on-skin grid you plan to test.

Ask your friend to close his or her eyes. Using the end of a broom bristle, gently touch the skin within each box of the grid on the back of your friend's hand. Instruct your friend to tell you whenever a touch is felt. For every box on the grid where your friend can feel a touch, use a plus sign (+) to mark the corresponding box on the grid in your science notebook. Do not mark boxes in the grid where no touch is felt.

In how many of the sixteen grid positions did your friend feel touch? About how far apart are the touch receptors on the back of your friend's hand?

Repeat the experiment for other parts of your friend's skin.

Which regions of the body seem to have the most touch receptors? Which seem to have the fewest touch receptors?

You can use the same grids to look for pain and temperature receptors in the next experiment.

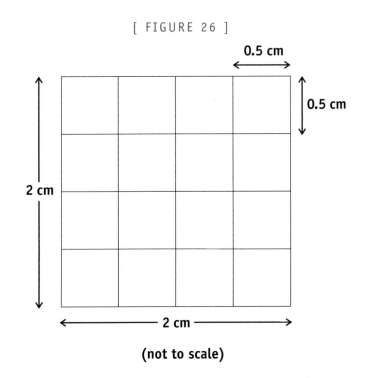

[FIGURE 26]

0.5 cm

0.5 cm

2 cm

2 cm

(not to scale)

Grids like the one shown here can be drawn on a subject's skin. Touch the center of each box in the grid with the end of a broom bristle. In which of the boxes are touch receptors found in the skin?

5.4 Perception of Temperature

Materials:
- 3 large bowls
- tap water (hot and cold)
- ice cubes
- clock or watch

There are sense receptors in your skin that respond to hot and cold. However, how you perceive temperature depends on the previous environment to which your sense receptors for temperature were exposed. This was first discovered by a German physiologist named Ernst Weber (1795–1878).

To begin this experiment, obtain three large bowls. To the first bowl add room-temperature tap water until the bowl is three-fourths full. Fill a second bowl about halfway with cold tap water. Add ice cubes until this bowl is also three-fourths full. Fill a third bowl to the same level with hot tap water. **As you add hot water to the bowl, test the water in the bowl with your hand. Be sure the water is not too hot. If it is, add some cold water until you are able to place your right hand in the water without discomfort.**

Place the three bowls side by side with the hot water on your right, the ice water on your left, and the room-temperature water in the middle. Dry your hands thoroughly. Then place your right hand in the hot water and your left hand in the ice water. Hold them under the water for 3 minutes.

After 3 minutes, remove your hands from the bowls and put both of them into the bowl of room-temperature water. How does your right hand perceive the water's temperature? How does your left hand perceive the water's temperature?

What does this experiment tell you about the way past experiences influence your perception of temperature?

Science Fair Project Idea

Place a large wooden object and a large metallic object side by side in the same room for an hour so that you know both objects are at the same temperature. Now touch first one object and then the other. Try to explain your perception of their temperatures being different.

Materials:
- a friend
- two 20-gram standard metal weights or two stacks of 6 pennies glued together
- warm (40°C, or 104°F) water and cup
- ice cube
- several people

Ernst Weber, the man who discovered that temperature receptors are not good thermometers, gave his name to the effect you will see in this experiment. The experiment will show how temperature can affect a person's perception of weight.

Ask a friend to lie on his or her back on the floor with eyes closed. Place on your friend's forehead, to one side, a standard 20-gram metal weight (or a stack of six pennies glued together) that has been in warm (40°C, or 104°F) water for several minutes. On the other side of the forehead place an identical 20-gram metal weight (or stack of pennies) that has been resting on an ice cube for the same length of time. Does your subject perceive the two objects to be equal in mass? If not, which one seems to weigh more?

Try the same experiment with a number of subjects. Are your results always the same? Can you offer an explanation for the way the weights are perceived?

🏆 5.6 Coins to Touch

Materials:
- coins: pennies, nickels, dimes, and quarters
- table
- a friend

There is touch and then there is multiple touch. The two can provide quite different information. To see what this means, put a variety of coins (pennies, nickels, dimes, and quarters) in your pocket. Close your eyes and put your hand in your pocket. Turn one of the coins in your fingers and try to identify it. Keeping your eyes closed, remove the coin and place it on a table. Continue this process until you think you have identified and placed on the table at least one coin of each type. Then open your eyes to see how well you have done. You probably did very well.

Now have a friend place the same coins on a table while you stand nearby with your eyes closed. Your friend will guide the tip of your index finger to the top of one of the coins so that you can touch it. Just touch it; do not manipulate it! Can you identify it?

Have your friend guide your finger to other coins. Try to identify the coins just by touching. How well did you do?

Touch alone provides very little information. But by manipulating the coins, you can construct a three-dimensional mental "picture" of the coins that will help you identify them. Just as you could identify coins by feeling them, so people who are blind can "see" a friend by running their hands over that person's face.

🏆 Science Fair Project Idea

Blindfold friends and ask them to identify common objects by feeling them with one hand. You might try such things as keys, pens, paper clips, coins, rulers, and others. How accurately can your friends identify items by touch? How well do a number of older people do when given the same task?

FURTHER READING

Books

Bochinski, Julianne Blair. *The Complete Workbook for Science Fair Projects.* Hoboken, N.J.: John Wiley and Sons, Inc., 2005.

Hayhurst, Chris. *The Brain and Spinal Cord: Learning How We Think, Feel and Move.* New York: The Rosen Publishing Group, Inc., 2002.

Moorman, Thomas. *How to Make Your Science Project Scientific.* Revised Edition. New York: John Wiley & Sons, Inc., 2002.

Sherman, Josepha. *The Ear: Learning How We Hear.* New York: The Rosen Publishing Group, Inc., 2002.

Silverstein, Alvin, Virginia Silverstein, and Laura Silverstein Nunn. *Touching and Feeling.* Brookfield, Conn.: Twenty-First Century Books, 2002.

Weise, Jim. *Head to Toe Science: Over 40 Eye-popping, Spine-tingling, Heart-pounding Activities that Teach Kids About the Human Body.* New York: John Wiley, 2000.

Internet Addresses

Chudler, Eric H. *Neuroscience for Kids.* 1996–2008.
<http://faculty.washington.edu/chudler/experi.html>.

Society for Science and the Public. *Science News for Kids.* 2008.
<http://www.sciencenewsforkids.org/pages/search.asp?catid=10>.

WGBH. *Zoom Sci.* 1998–2006.
<http://pbskids.org/zoom/activities/sci/>.

INDEX

31901047427457